# THE MOST DANGEROUS BUSINESS BOOK

## YOU'LL EVER READ

**Gregory Hartley**
**Maryann Karinch**

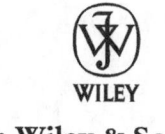

WILEY

John Wiley & Sons, Inc.

Published by John Wiley & Sons, Inc., Hoboken, New Jersey.
Published simultaneously in Canada.

For general information on our other products and services or for technical support, please contact our Customer Care Department within the United States at (800) 762-2974, outside the United States at (317) 572-3993 or fax (317) 572-4002.

Wiley also publishes its books in a variety of electronic formats. Some content that appears in print may not be available in electronic books. For more information about Wiley products, visit our web site at www.wiley.com.

**Library of Congress Cataloging-in-Publication Data:**
Hartley, Gregory.
    The most dangerous business book you'll ever read / Gregory Hartley & Maryann Karinch.
      p. cm.
    ISBN 978-0-470-88802-5 (cloth)
    ISBN 978-1-118-00172-1 (ebk)
    ISBN 978-1-118-00173-8 (ebk)
    ISBN 978-1-118-00174-5 (ebk)
      1. Success in business.   2. Interpersonal relations.   3. Career development.
I. Karinch, Maryann.  II. Title.
    HF5386.H2746 2011
    650.1—dc22

                                    2010034741

Printed in the United States of America

SKY10021039_092120

*To my son, Jeffrey*
*—Greg Hartley*

*To Mom, Karl, and Jim*
*—Maryann Karinch*

# CONTENTS

# FOREWORD

I first met Greg quite a few years ago while running a corporate sales and management simulation training program called "War Games" that created the true stress and unpredictability of real-life sales and management opportunities—our version of firing live ammo over the heads of our sales and management workforce. Greg joined me to prep our actors in their various roles as customers, protagonists, and antagonists. His expertise in reading people and interrogation was key to the development and constant improvement of our war games sales and management training. Over years of running these simulations, Greg would often amaze me in the first hour of day 1 of these three-day events. He would point at folks across the room and predict their outcome. "He's going to be in tears by day two; she's going to do awesome under stress; get the janitor to follow him with a mop and bucket—he's nauseous nervous." He was frighteningly accurate. All of this just by watching how they projected themselves, how they interrelated with one another, and what their posture was. Greg was on my team to ensure each student got full benefit of the experience.

They did.

This book takes the tools of military intelligence such as heightened observation skills, deliberate interpersonal interactions, and a Special Forces–like bias for action and relates their potential value to the business world today. The metaphor of business leaders as intelligence assets using finely honed skills, tools, and a deliberate backbone to advance their companies in a vision that business is war drives home some key realities. If you are not aware of tools such as these in this book, how do you know if they aren't being used on you daily? Are you already tied to a chair with a spotlight in your face and just not aware? Or, are you a novice at some of these techniques with occasional success in using them to your company's advantage? Perhaps you are not yet aware of many of these approaches—at least not in a business context.

This book goes a long way in detailing the value of taking the lead and deliberately advancing through behaviors long known to be successful on the battlefield and behind its lines. Victory to a winning organization is most often the result of the successful execution of strategies that can be very subtle, very engaging, yet very effective. Being in control of each encounter and knowing what is really going on while the interaction is occurring is a key ingredient of victory. Identifying behaviors that are antagonistic or even covert and then knowing how to act upon them is a clear path to victory.

Personally, I want to thank Greg and Maryann for this book. In my view, it successfully marries the tools of intelligence and special operations with frequent opportunities for business advancement. While I read the manuscript, I flashed back to the many late-night meetings Greg and I had watching our very tired sales and management "plebes" struggle through the high-stress encounters of business interactions we set up for them in our controlled environment. Then I think about how much better they later performed in the business world for having gone through it and having learned some of these tools.

The Buddhist proverb "When the student is ready, the teacher will appear" likely was never meant to apply to the business world, but I find it haunting how many times a practice used every day somewhere is new and interesting in a different context such as business. Who among us hasn't struggled to find approaches and answers to situations only to find what we were looking for already exists in an alternate universe? This book will help you identify and put into practice techniques that are already successful in our intelligence community.

—Louis J. Zaccone
Regional Executive, Trane

# ACKNOWLEDGMENTS

### Greg Hartley

Thanks to Lou Zaccone for writing the foreword. Jim, I don't know what we would do without you. Dina, I really appreciate your patience while I am tied up in this process. Maryann, this relationship continues to improve and make the process easier—thanks. Rick Croley, many of my ideas would stay in my head if I didn't talk with you about them; thanks for the friendship. Rick and Karen, you have been more family than friends to me; Karen, this year you have been a lifesaver—thank you. Dan and the staff at John Wiley & Sons, Inc., this is a pleasure; thanks for reaching out to us.

### Maryann Karinch

With great thanks to my brother and father, both noble Marines; they contributed to my appreciation of discipline, planning, and understanding of Semper Fidelis. They prepared me amply to develop strong relationships with teammates, training partners, and colleagues in the military community as well as the civilian intelligence community—most notably Greg Hartley, whom I respect greatly as both a military man and a businessman. I cherish our partnership. I also want to thank several mentors who, like Greg, built on their military/intelligence expertise to drive their career success. Primary among them are four of my coauthors: Peter Earnest, Dean Hohl, Peter Spevak, and Patrick Avon. Sincere thanks to Lou Zaccone for the wonderful foreword. A big thanks to Jim McCormick and Michael Dobson, both for keen insights throughout the development of the book and for their patient listening.

I am also very grateful to Dan Ambrosio and Ashley Allison at John Wiley & Sons, Inc., and to other members of the Wiley team who will be helping us down the road. Your enthusiasm and professionalism are extraordinary.

# INTRODUCTION

If you ask, "Can I?" then you will not get far in using the skills covered in this book.

If you ask, "Why?" "How?" or "Why not?" then you can excel in applying them.

When I teach, I know someone who asks the question, "Tell me how to do *x*" probably has limited ability to integrate the set of skills I'm sharing. "What do you think of doing *x* in this situation?" is a much better question. It suggests that the person asking it has a sense of putting the tools and techniques into context.

Although the skills have their roots in military and civilian intelligence practices, even intelligence professionals don't necessarily know how to use them in business. If they did, they would all get great business jobs when they leave the intelligence community. Here's why most of them do not: You can know a lot about techniques to read and manipulate human behavior, but unless you can apply them in the context of day-to-day human interaction, your opportunities will be seriously limited.

It takes courage to be good in business. Many intelligence professionals would not recognize the parallel demands of their life and yours or the fact that excellence in business does take guts. Business is a purposeful activity, just like freeing hostages and collecting intelligence to win a war. Applying extreme interpersonal skills in encounters with enemies and criminals is essentially no different from applying them in a meeting, negotiation, or ongoing business challenge.

You have a fundamental and pervasive challenge that most intelligence collectors do not. Many live outside of their target's scrutiny, whereas you live within the scrutiny of the people you will use these skills on. Being a full-time intelligence officer does not mean always being in harm's way, but in a sense, you are. Many intelligence professionals gather and/or analyze intelligence during the day and then go home at night just as you do. Others are full-time intelligence collectors, dropping in and out of their areas of operation around the clock. You are more like the second type—full time all of the time—because your coworkers and competitors are the people you are targeting. You also get a few advantages they don't, though, such as your knowledge of how business functions, your ability to move freely and conspicuously within that environment with mandate, and a holistic look at the tools in intelligence instead of one specialty.

Ask yourself why you want to master the skills of a profiler, polygrapher, spy, interrogator, negotiator, analyst, or expert in special operations? You probably have multiple reasons relating to your professional development, but list one that ties your reason to your company.

The dynamics of all organisms are self-sustaining. That's true whether the organism is organic or not. Government exists to produce government. Business exists to produce business. Organisms know how to take care of themselves. The greatest strength comes from within. And in most cases, so does their greatest weakness.

Back to the question: Why do you want these skills? Do you intend to apply them for the good of your company, or will you use them to become the weakness within?

Only a double agent or a disgruntled psychopath would respond yes to the latter part of the question. And yet, if you use these skills *without a plan*—at all times—you may well become the weakness within. Not only that, but you could kill your own career.

You would be a disaster in business if you wrapped yourself perpetually in the aura of a "dangerous" businessperson because you have studied the skills in this book. You are sophisticated with the skills only if you can turn them off and project an aura that's appropriate for the occasion.

Understand why and when the tools are necessary. If you exercise use on an ad hoc basis just to test the results, aside from possibly hurting your company, you will get your ass handed to you by a savvier person in your company. Use these skills with purpose.

In helping a company through a politically charged acquisition, I saw what happens when a person fails to apply the interpersonal skills covered in this book. He chooses the wrong allies, relies on contaminated information, and narrows his options. He causes team members to slam into each other. The result: career death. It may be a slow death, but the end is still in sight.

Your company does not have to go through a merger or acquisition for you to need these skills. Everyday office politics demand that you know how to assess personalities, network effectively, ask solid questions and analyze the responses, and hold the advantage in any meeting or negotiation. I've watched many business executives sabotage themselves by lacking expertise in those areas, and I will give you true stories to spotlight how to avoid their disasters.

For example, Glen had lined up his career path to head straight for a division manager slot. If he reached it, he could earn bonuses and perks that would keep him very happy until retirement. He played by the rules and stuck close to his boss, another consummate rule-follower. When new management moved Glen's boss to another department, Glen still believed he had a shot at the division manager position because he had a solid performance record. New management saw it differently. Glen's upward climb in the company hinged on one major relationship—the one with his boss. He had no network of supporters; he never cultivated one. Glen's track record showed he had a by-the-book approach. But the new people at the top decided to throw out that book. They had no reason to believe that Glen could adapt to the changes as well as other people in line for the job.

When many people are jockeying for position, one of the biggest mistakes you can make is paying attention to your own horse. You forget there are other horses on the track and don't see them overtaking you along the side.

What Glen did was get on his horse, ride it as hard as he could, and crack his whip at anyone who came close to him without looking to see who was coming up on the outside. He invested all of his faith in the idea that his horse would win.

Glen failed in multiple ways—ways that will become clear in the upcoming pages. To name a few failures, he did not establish rapport, demonstrate his value to the right audience, analyze options, or uncover hidden agendas. Learning how to sort personalities and ask good questions, along with other abilities, will help prevent that kind of professional disaster—and the exercises in this book will help you hone your skills. You will gain a repertoire of skills that you can use to fast-track your career.

You have countless opportunities to use the information in this book to dramatically alter how your company does business. Simple example: I told one company to change the image they wanted to feature in trade magazine advertising. The man in the picture was supposed to exude confidence, specifically confidence in the solution the company provided him. I saw disdain. The knit brow and upturned head did not project a positive look. Subliminally, prospective customers who saw it could get the message, "He doesn't think this product is good enough for him." If you have a grasp on substance like that, you are dangerous. The danger is that you have something that other people do not: the ability to read and manipulate human behavior.

In developing the book, our principle source of information was experience—experience with the types of professionals featured in the book and experience applying the tools in business.

I have served as an active military interrogator assigned to a Special Forces unit, an interrogation instructor in SERE (Survival, Evasion, Resistance, and Escape) working alongside Rangers, Special Forces, and Delta Force soldiers. I have run multinational joint force interrogation and counterintelligence exercises, and I have served on missions with Special Ops folks from all branches of the U.S. Armed Forces. I was also inserted in the Saudi and Kuwaiti armies in the first Gulf War. In addition, I've taught law enforcement specialists, nonmilitary intelligence experts, attorneys, and businesspeople and have worked alongside profilers, negotiators, and polygraphers.

Maryann has experience training with SEALs, Rangers, and Marines, as well as experience working on projects with former clandestine officers for the Central Intelligence Agency (CIA). She is a two-time Eco-Challenge competitor and knows a thing or two about Special Ops–style team building from endurance racing and skydiving with people from the worlds of military and civilian intelligence.

What allowed me the opportunity to work with all of these teams was the ability to read people and influence behavior. In working with these disparate teams, I learned one main thing: All of the skills needed by *you* or an intelligence resource are the same. I call them Extreme Interpersonal Skills. This core skill suite is tied closely to every intelligence job in the business.

Note that these are not all of the skills that exist in intelligence. They are the skills I understand, and the ones that apply to business. So, although some intelligence resources plant or sweep for listening devices, spy tradecraft like that is neither useful/legal nor within my realm of expertise.

The intelligence business is made up of all kinds of human beings who come from various walks of life. Some are right out of high school; others are successful business professionals. They create an amalgam of personalities and abilities. The skills they have in common are featured in this book, but filtered through my eyes and explained in a way that will be meaningful to you. The ultimate proof of the applicability and effectiveness in your world is that I use them in business every day.

What the diversity of people in the intelligence communities highlights is that people aren't born spies or negotiators. The skills development process cultivates that expertise. And that is why I know that, armed with your plan for using them, you can master them in your business environment.

I see a lot of people who wander into work with precisely the same set of behaviors and demeanor they have with their friends at a baseball game. It's the same behavior they have at home with their kids. Maybe it's the same behavior they have at church. They miss the requirements of success: Match your behavior and skills to the requirements of the situation.

Some people at work do not know you at all. Some of them know you a little bit. Who are you to those people? How would you like them to perceive you?

If you want to engender a perception of you as strong, capable, or even dangerous, you have to do that methodically, orchestrating your use of the skills in this book. You should not read this book and want to change who you are, though. Build on what you have and who you are. You have permission to reach further than you may think you do. I write to teach you to think about how these skills fit into your life. I cannot make them fit your life— *you* can.

Start by getting the answers to these questions clear in your head: What are your purposes and goals? Who are your natural allies and enemies? More important, who are your potential allies and enemies?

Business is war between your company and one or more other companies. I've had people counter that by saying that those other companies are also potential allies and that there are many ways they work together to improve the industry. That is one part of the equation. Just remember that allies may help you occasionally, but that doesn't mean they put your needs above theirs. Harden up: Your competition is taking money out of your pocket. That makes them the enemy. That means you need to train to win.

"It is better to be feared than loved, if you cannot be both."
—*Niccolo Machiavelli*

# CHAPTER 1

# Sort Personalities Like a Profiler

## Tools
• Disposition matrix
• Action matrix

W hen you think of profiling, *Silence of the Lambs* might come to mind. In the movie, you see members of the Behavioral Analysis Unit of the Federal Bureau of Investigation (FBI) try to piece together the traits of a serial killer. As the movie progresses, the team narrows the options of what kind of person could commit such heinous crimes and why he would commit them. These profilers look at demographic information and trends and then target where that person might be found.

The kind of profiling I do, and what I will teach you to do, uses the reverse of that process. Instead of using past behavior to narrow down options about an individual we're looking for, we will create a profile of someone we're observing. The purpose is not only to understand with whom we're dealing but also to predict that person's response to a given specific stimulus and thereby influence that person's behavior.

You will use profiling skills the way I used them as an interrogator and the way I now use them daily in business since leaving the intelligence field.

## Value to Business

You can learn to sort personality types so well that you can often predict how a person will address a crisis, face conflict, or handle a negotiation, for example. When you know the personality profile of your colleague, boss, customer, or competitor, you are in a position to:

• Predict what that person will do in a given situation
• Manipulate that person
• Predict outcomes

In later chapters, I'll add insights on identifying stimuli that cause stress, how a person behaves and talks when relaxed, and much more. Put them together and you have a skill set that puts you in control in many environments and meetings.

The same is true for knowing the personality of a group. Even though the individuals in the group have different profiles, when they come together, they might assume a set of traits that drive behavior. For example, you might have a customer you could aptly describe as self-centered and indifferent; that customer as a whole also focuses on the flaws in a product and the deficits in service. At the same time, your contact at the organization may have a contrasting set of traits. Or you may see that, year after year, your company's customer service department projects a caring and positive attitude; they put the reputation of the company above their individual tendencies when dealing with customers. Again, knowing the personality of the group will help you predict how the group will act, which will give you powerful insights into how to change one of the group's practices or processes.

One of the things you hear today from human resources professionals and a lot of team-building coaches is, "Don't put people in boxes."

Wrong. Put them in well-defined boxes—specifically the ones I introduce you to in this chapter. Just make sure you have a firm grasp of why you put them in particular boxes; then use this understanding of where individuals fit to create better coalitions and create cooperation.

As you read along, think about whether or not the traits your team demonstrates are aligned to your goals as a company. If not, you will need to adjust so that you align your organization and intent. As you read this chapter, start to categorize people. The ability to do that is a foundation skill you will need for manipulation, networking, and team building, all of which are covered in later chapters.

## Natural Profilers

Profiling might sound like a skill requiring straightforward analytic skills, but in fact, the people inclined to do it well are those who see patterns, correlations, and trends.

People who make correlations easily have a higher ratio of white matter to gray matter in their brains than the dominantly gray matter folks. In his March 2008 *Scientific American* article "White Matter Matters," Neuroscientist R. Douglas Fields explained succinctly what the difference is: "White matter, long thought to be passive tissue, actively affects how the brain learns and dysfunctions. Although gray matter (composed of neurons) does the brain's thinking and calculating, white matter (composed of myelin-coated axons) controls the signals that neurons share, coordinating how well brain regions work together."

People with more gray matter than white matter, then, tend to be great with isolated facts; on the extreme of that group are autistics. Those of us who are good at tying ideas together see trends and tend to be good at strategic thinking. We also make better liars than the high gray matter folks.

A high gray matter person would understand absolutes and get the details right but would not necessarily understand easily how the details fit together or tied in with everyday information. Put her through an exercise in which she would have to lie about writing a book about biology, for example, and she could go only so far before it was clear she didn't know enough to write a book about biology. On the other hand, the white matter person would be able to link the few facts he knew to something relevant in daily life and move you off topic.

People who are good at that can get away with a lot. They can demonstrate value easily and forge connections quickly. They are also predisposed to be good profilers.

## Tools of Profiling

Sorting people in terms of character traits is an essential step in understanding how to get leverage with them. Identifying the way they take action and process information strengthens your ability to converse with and question them.

The upcoming sections give you a new way of profiling yourself, members of your team, and your team/company as a whole by considering the following:

- Disposition is about an individual's relationship with her world.
- Action styles describe the level of energy a person tends to commit to action and how he handles time.

As part of that discussion, you will see how these traits play out in the four "help categories," which express how a person relates to groups, and the four "type categories," which capture how a person relates to the system, whether that means how the team works or how the whole company works.

At the end of the discussion, you will have a fresh perspective on yourself as well as other people on your team. You will have answers to questions such as, "Why do we seem to disagree all the time?" or "Why don't we have any momentum?"

The tools covered here enable you to make accurate assessments and predictions of behavior in many situations. And they give you valuable insights to know when and how to push someone to get what you want.

When you're through with this section, do not feel a need to remember the words I used to describe the traits. What you want to do is this:

- Remember the concepts.
- Think about pros and cons of each in a business environment.
- Stay alert for examples of how the character traits operate in a continuum.

- Let your mind explore the vulnerabilities associated with each of the traits.

To begin, let's do some reverse engineering. Think about the major traits of the person featured in this story:

> Joel heard about a village in Africa with no local source of potable water. He went there immediately armed with plans for a well. Recruiting semiskilled workers from the nearest city, he put them to work building the well and paid them out of his own pocket. When the well became functional, he left Africa and returned home. Assuming he had saved the village, he felt good about his actions and never looked back. Unfortunately, the workers from the city had introduced a disease into the population of the village that proved fatal to the indigenous people. Most eventually died.

What makes a person clearly out for the good of his fellow human miss such a vital piece of information? What about him allows him to set in motion a chain of events that has the opposite effect he intended? This is far more than an issue of lacking common sense.

I have learned how to put people in boxes to understand—and predict—behavior so that outcomes like this are very often not a surprise. This is the system of profiling I am introducing to you here.

My system of sorting people in terms of character traits comes out of extensive empirical research that began even before my years as an interrogator. It is based on information synergized after years of working in intelligence, the Army as a whole, business, TV news analysis, construction management, and labor, as well as from a psychology education, raising animals, and just plain living.

Why does that detail matter here? When I was an interrogator, I learned to use fourteen approved approaches—the same ones being discussed in the media daily in the wake of the interrogation scandals around the civilized world. These were simple levers: If he demonstrates *xyz* behavior, then use these psychological ploys. Young interrogators all over the world learn these tools and, as a result of relying on them alone, have some success with prisoners.

"Some success" never seemed quite good enough to me. I couldn't simply say, "This works pretty well" and leave it at that. My mind often pondered the next question: "Why?" This is the questioning that ultimately led me to a unique way of analyzing how people fit into society.

In sharing this information with you, I hope to get you to assimilate what is useful from it into your own repertoire of analysis skills. The important caveat is that the material here is an introduction to the concepts. Apply it and it will take your interactions with people to a new level, but keep in mind there is a lot more where this came from.

## Values and Ego

In any culture, certain traits will be celebrated openly and therefore trumpeted as virtue. For instance, selfless public service in the United States has been hailed as a virtue. Many renowned figures have demonstrated so-called selfless service up to, and including, martyrdom. Look at Robert and John F. Kennedy; Martin Luther King, Jr.; or any of a long list of people in the public eye who are celebrated for giving their very lives in their efforts to build a better society. On a much closer-to-home level, the fêted American work ethic is exactly that same type of selfless service. Neither the actions of the famous American martyrs nor those of the people who "keep their noses to the grindstone" are born of pure virtue, but both deliver what the culture needs and are therefore celebrated as virtue.

In contrast, we have traits that are not celebrated, but they certainly are rewarded. When a culture rewards such behaviors, people growing up in that culture get mixed messages. For example, consider the trait that ostensibly stands as the "black" to the "white" of selflessness: selfishness. Instead of working long work hours because of the nobility of hard work, you do it with intent to climb quickly, and over the slow people, up the corporate ladder. But if you are holding this book, you already understand the value of this trait and the potential rewards of cultivating it.

And so although selfishness is not celebrated as a virtue, it is certainly a core element of our society. While we might celebrate the selflessness, the United States, France, Germany, Japan, or any other industrialized nation would not have occurred without both selflessness and its counterpart. We have benefited from having both edges of the sword in play.

I mention this for two reasons. First, any person can take a celebrated value to the point of a self-defining character trait. A person can start off with selfless service as intent only because an event spurs that person to action, just as the kidnapping and murder of Adam Walsh set his parents on a campaign that resulted in three different laws related to child protection. But with time, actions like this can become deeply rooted in self and define the very core of the individual. When this happens, the real driver is no longer the service for its own sake but the need to keep large piles of fuel on the hot-burning ego. This is not to say it is all bad. Once the celebrated value becomes ego-defining, the person pours even more passion into the defining trait and the results are more of what the culture celebrates. So when the trait becomes a definition, it moves to ego and the person now places his heart mind and soul to accomplishing exactly whatever the goal is. *Note well:* In this way he has moved to exactly the same position as the ego-driven climber. In other words, he has *moved from value to ego.*

Does the opposite occur?

Yes, and that is the second thing to remember. Out of the egotistical action of climbing the corporate ladder, the person fuels economy or other organizational growth, creating opportunity for other people. She surrounds herself with other successful people who directly or indirectly contribute to society through their actions. She therefore becomes much more like the selfless service person. Actions made possible by selfishness cause the impetus itself to be celebrated as virtue or rewarded (even if maligned) and to become defining for a culture. Case in point: Bill Gates, one of the most renowned capitalists of all time, plans to spend $3 billion on education sometime between 2010 and 2017, and one of the other most renowned capitalists of all time, Warren Buffet, is going to help him do it.

In either case, these defining movements of virtue or ego can become so ingrained in behaviors that the full-blown practitioner has defined herself; any move away from the trait is more endangering to the self than death. I refer to this kind of "fate worse than death" as *personal extinction.*

### Disposition Matrix

In the mix of sorting styles and temperament indices available to you from a variety of sources, you will find that many are complex and unwieldy when you try to use them in a business environment. I believe you will find my system immediately helpful in understanding the people with whom you do business. You will use it to tag them and put them into boxes.

First of all, get it out of your head that any of these traits is good or bad. I want you to look at the circular nature of human thought and behavior rather than judge the merits of traits like selflessness and selfishness.

Most of the tools described throughout this book are based on finding similarities between you and other people and bonding with them or finding differences between you and fracturing from them. The tools of profiling will help you think about people in a way that makes that process clear and relatively easy to implement.

There are obvious political examples of each of the types in these charts, and for clarity's sake, I will often use political examples to illustrate my thoughts. Regardless of what person I might be talking about, realize that one is not by design better or worse than another; they just have different outcomes. I do have a very strong opinion about which of those outcomes are desirable and good for business, though. I would say that, as you read the charts, try to think about where you fit and why. Then consider how opposed you are to certain people when you disagree with them. With that in mind, see where you think they fit on the chart. Often the disagreement comes out of someone else being so much like you, and yet manifesting the same trait in a very different way. They are like the other side of your coin. Due to this circular nature of the traits, the more radical you become in your practice of the trait, the closer you come to your opposite.

I introduce the system with a two-axis matrix because we have all had exposure to the model (see Figure 1.1). On the $x$-axis, you see Selfish versus Altruistic; on the $y$-axis, Individual versus Collectivist.

### Selfish versus Altruistic: Focus on Altruistic With Mother
Teresa at the head of the pack, our modern culture celebrates

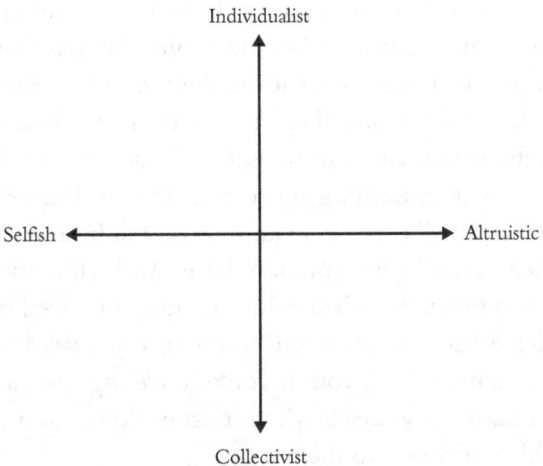

**FIGURE 1.1**   The axes feature opposite traits. When taken to the extreme, each trait can become its opposite.

altruists. Altruism means putting the good of others, whether collectively or individually, ahead of self. By definition, then, altruism involves noble acts.

When you read these contrasting words, you automatically want to be associated with the altruist, don't you? Ask yourself why. Is altruism in itself a desirable quality? It may be celebrated in our society to the point of virtue, but do you feel you belong in a tribe of altruists? Or is altruistic behavior simply a way to gain the admiration of those around you? If the latter is true, you are tied to the connotation of the word and not the actual meaning.

If you want the rewards of being an altruist, you'll act like one. If society punished you for behaving that way, you might be a lot less inclined to exhibit altruism or you might be driven to it by the feeling of persecution. Patterns of reward and punishment for behavior create what is the norm for the individual; actions that a person takes nominally for the good of others might be so self-fulfilling that the real reason to keep doing it is that it will hurt to stop doing it. If you're a celebrity getting heaps of accolades in the tabloids for volunteering to help orphans, you don't want to taint your reputation by making the orphans someone else's problem.

Remember that moving too far in the direction of altruist will make you selfish eventually, as I've described the continuum here. If Joe volunteers at the homeless shelter one night a week while his wife is at Yoga class, is his action inherently "better than" hers? Now imagine our hero Joe likes the feeling he gets from helping those poor, less fortunate souls at the shelter, so he starts to volunteer three days a week and then five, until he no longer has time for his family. Is that altruism the same virtue you would want to celebrate, or is it something more akin to selfishness? Take that *x*-axis and wrap it all the way around in 3-D fashion until it comes back on itself. That's what you have here. And while the homeless might really appreciate Joe's altruism, he might be well on the way to be homeless himself. Joe needs to listen to the wisdom of flight attendants when they tell you, if you're traveling with a child, put the oxygen mask on yourself when it drops down, and then put it on the child. Selfishness to the rescue.

On the healthy end, the person realizes altruism is defining for him and decides to make his life's work helping others, he works his way up Maslow's Hierarchy of Needs, belonging to the group of do-gooders and then differentiating himself to sainthood, finding along the way a good balance between satisfaction of his needs and the good he does for others (see Figure 1.2).

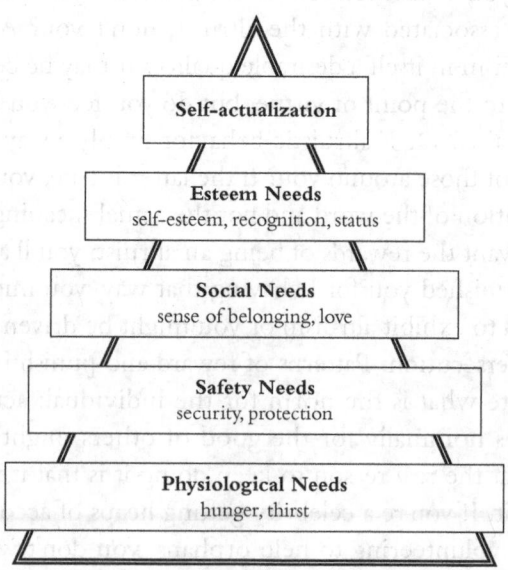

FIGURE 1.2   Maslow's Hierarchy of Needs. Most of us move between the third and fourth levels: belonging and differentiating.
*Source:* Maslow, Abraham (1954). *Motivation and Personality.* New York: Harper. p. 236.

On the unhealthy end, the person is the martyr of the group, constantly sacrificing and living the meager life of the unrecognized—right out in the open. The sheer pleasure derived from knowing he has been wronged by being overlooked all the time he has been there to help others is his definition.

Each of these comes with its own challenges in a business environment. When you are dealing with the well-adjusted person, his definition of altruism is intricately woven with the idea. If you do anything to throw off his feeling of self and his self-identification as a defender and protector, you toy with his wrath, as well as that of people who benefit from his good deeds. Rather than challenge him, if you can mobilize him to the good of the organization or team, you get all of his commitment and influence behind your objective. Once he is "on cause," rest assured it will be done.

Regarding an altruist's long-suffering "martyr" side, be careful not to upset the status quo unintentionally. Asking the person to participate in something for the good of others will likely get the response you desire, and as you do it, recognize that "he's been there for the long haul for all of us."

What happens if your so-called altruist won't play nicely? Bring out the selfish person in him. Assign him annoying or trivial tasks "for the good of others" that will make him object and force him to show his true selfish identity.

**Selfish versus Altruistic: Focus on Selfish** I use selfish as a category, so I ask you to move yourself away from the negative connotations of the word. Selfishness is by definition the opposite of altruism. It carries pejorative meaning in our society and yet it should not, because a truly altruistic act cannot be carried out unless the person doing it has a firm grasp of, and respect for, self. The teachings of various religions are full of such self-awareness lessons. Jesus didn't say, "Oh, what the heck, I'll be a big hero if I die on the cross today, so let's get on with it." In the time before his crucifixion, Jesus asked, "Let O father if it be possible this cup pass from me" (Matthew 26). That's an act of self. But he continued, "Nevertheless not as I will but as you will." Would this act of sacrifice have the same meaning without the line indicating that he may not view this as an ideal situation?

Humans have a self-preservation instinct and some of us are designed to be more competitive about it than others. This desire to win and promote self is the way I define selfish here. As I said, we fit somewhere on a continuum, so most are more aligned to self or more aligned to altruism—and most not at the extreme.

Unlike the altruist, the selfish person is more focused on outcomes for her (individually) or her own (collectively). She takes actions that are focused on outcomes that mean something to her or her organization. She might take negative steps against others, but more often the negative outcomes for others are outcroppings of positive actions for self.

On the healthy side, the selfish person is concerned with promotions, growth opportunities, and being seen as more competent than others. With a sense of self-respect, she is driven to outpace or outshine her competitors, whether individual or organization. It isn't mean spirited; she just wants to do well.

On the unhealthy side, the selfish person is envious of others moving ahead of her and uses whatever it takes to prevent that. She constantly looks at others as stepping stones and has no genuine interest in teamwork. She becomes toxic because she cannot let others pass her. She uses all of her energy to sabotage others or to take credit for their work.

**Altruistic and Selfish**   Few people sit far to the left on the selfish axis, or far to the right as an altruist. Most take a spot on a bench somewhere in the middle.

Stop for a minute and assign yourself or others to the radial diagram in Figure 1.3.

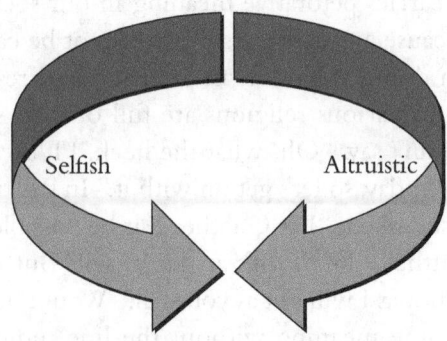

FIGURE 1.3   Where are you on the continuum?

**Individual versus Collectivist**  Americans identify with individualism. We often talk of the rugged individualists in American history, and yet, if we look closely we find those protagonists far from individualists. We may admire cowboys in classic Westerns while simultaneously finding them arrogant and insensitive.

When we describe someone as individualistic, the positive bent is "a person who does what he wants to do." But as a society, we are the first to sign up, join in, and give of ourselves. Most Americans want to belong to a group and then to show their identity by points of difference. This is fundamentally no different from any other group, large or small, in the world.

In the mid-1990s, I was in a country bar in the outskirts of Washington, DC, with a British naval intelligence officer. We were watching people line dance when the young man looked at me and said, "Good God, your people freed the world from socialism and now I see you here dancing like a flock of sheep." I pointed out to him that, while we as a nation are so radically opposed to a government foisted on folks that tells them what to do, we as a culture are avid joiners. You see evidence of this in so many aspects of our daily life—how we eat, what sports we like, what churches we attend, and what celebrities we think are hot. Most Americans would define their lives as very individualist until forced to isolate the points of difference in their lives.

In a general sense, individualists believe that only when a person is implementing her own desires and plans of action can the group as whole succeed; anything else is a slow death for the group. Pure individualists believe a person has the right to make decisions about not only what she wears but also about everything she does. Of course, the sane person immediately asks, "Where's the limit?"

And so, in a society like America, limits by peer group or government start to affect what the individualist can get away with. Individualists on the sane side understand that one cannot take opinions to the extreme without becoming a collectivist. That is, I'm a cowboy who stands up for what's right no matter what . . . and by the way, it's in your best interests to agree with me. A dictator is the ultimate in individualists; he is not concerned about whether others agree and will resolutely pursue his agenda. Checks and balances are important to prevent individualists from becoming despots.

On the healthy side, an individualist sees everyone's voice as vital. Every person should have the right to do and contribute as he pleases. He might take an altruistic or a selfish approach. If he bends toward altruism, he sees value in allowing people to do as they see fit; he uses his resources to support their right of self-expression for the greater good. If selfish, he sees it his right to use skills and resources for his own good.

Collectivists believe that looking out for the group's good is the most important action they can take and that individuals will find fulfillment in satisfying group needs. The collectivist who sees the other person's point of view realizes that collectivist ideals need to be curbed to allow groups to grow. In contrast, those who cannot see others' points of view will have a tendency to create great reform movements that smother all other ideas out of existence, stagnate the culture, and create its ultimate death.

On a radial scale moving from left to right, a collectivist can go so far left that he creates culture that imposes one person's will on all others. By the same token, if an individualist goes too far in the opposite direction, he creates a culture in which the strongest of the group dominate and collectivism is inevitable. In this way the two extremes mimic each other (see Figure 1.4).

On a scale of 1 to 10, where 10 is far to the right, most of us fit somewhere in the middle, even if we would identify ourselves as an individualist or a collectivist. Mitigating factors like the laws of society and workplace rules also affect our decisions and prevent us from being an absolutist in either direction.

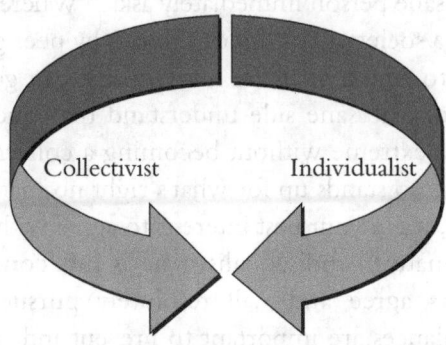

FIGURE 1.4    Where are you on the continuum?

## The Categories of Disposition

I sort all people into four easy-to-follow categories. Each category has degrees, of course, but you'll find them broadly applicable both to everyday life and to your business life. I apply a simple criterion for this assessment: HELP. As in, "Let me help you with that," or "You have to suck it up and help yourself." The closer to each of these four corner extremes a person gets, the more emotional and demonstrative she will be when dealing with others. As you look at Figure 1.5, note that this is about mind-set, not activity.

The closer you are to any given line, the more balanced on that axis you are.

**HELP MEs** The HELP MEs see group good as the prime driver in their world; more important, they see their piece of the group good as the driver. They can be high-level people who see benefit from the collectivist action or low-level people who gain from the

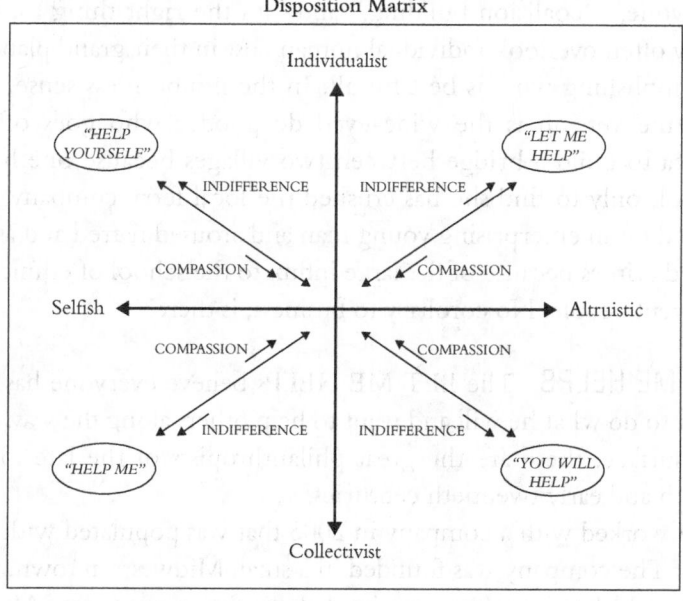

Disposition Matrix

FIGURE 1.5   HELP ME. Group good for my sake.
YOU WILL HELP. Group good at all costs.
LET ME HELP. Group good starts with me.
HELP YOURSELF. Group good comes from "watch out for number one."

same actions. For example, if everyone on the team pulls together and exceeds the sales quota, the boss may get the greatest reward, but everybody wins in some way.

Competence can play a part, but it doesn't have to. It simply means the person wants to gain from all people eating from a common bowl. It can be any level of business. It could be as simple as a conflict-averse peer asking for team presentations to allow him to outshine you and get the boss to see your ugly baby. It can also be the person who cannot pull his own weight getting others involved. They are closely linked to the altruistic collectivist and one can easily become the other.

**YOU WILL HELPS**  Altruistic collectivists believe in the good of the group and that there must be a better way for all concerned. Inevitably they organize a plan for improvement, along the way gaining the "support" of all parties. Depending on the action style of this type, she can move heaven or hell to get to the end results. The YOU WILL HELPs use phrases such as "this is a win–win for everyone," "coalition building," and "it's the right thing to do." They often overlook individual human cost in their grand plan for accomplishing what is best for all. In the nonbusiness sense, the extreme version is the wide-eyed do-gooder who goes off to Africa to build a bridge between two villages because one has a school, only to find she has crushed the local ferry company just started by an enterprising young man and aroused hatred and associated crimes because of the large influx to the school of ethnically different people. No corollary to business, is there?

**LET ME HELPS**  The LET ME HELPs believe everyone has the right to do what he will and want to help others along the way. On the surface, these are the great philanthropists of the late nineteenth and early twentieth centuries.

I worked with a company in 2005 that was populated with the type. The company was founded in a small Midwestern town, and the world headquarters remained there for many years. After a larger company bought out the other one, as you might expect, there were shifts in the organization. I was on the operations side of the business and regularly dealing with long-time employees who did things for the company that were unrelated to their job descriptions. When anyone on the business side from the large company decided to push on the IT/Support/Technical people and force them to do a project, those people would lock down and make it difficult for anyone to move forward. They had a "chip in" kind of mentality, which meant they went above and beyond and gave freely of their time if they wanted to—but not if they were forced to do something. This was especially true if they were told to do something by the folks who didn't really know what kind of help the company needed.

**HELP YOURSELFS**  Selfish individualists are cowboys. They want to do things their way, pass or fail, and you should do the same. They believe in hard work—or not—since the counterpart to the cowboy is the drifter. They see the world as a place that should allow for a person to make it on her own or fall on her face. They often use phrases like "pull yourself up; dust yourself off." You might immediately excuse this as nonexistent in business, but most organizations have cowboys in them and they bring a lot to the table. They do things their own way, often bringing a different perspective to the discussion; "innovation" is more than a buzzword to them. The reality is that no one is an island in business, so they drag others along in their success, in effect becoming more altruistic than they might realize. In balance they remind us of what's possible, in contrast to continuing with the way we have always done it. Out of balance, they bring us things like the Enron debacle.

Of course, there are boundary-line types as well and people who cannot make a commitment to anything specific and vacillate with the latest trend. Treat this as an introduction to a way of classifying people into cooperation categories, to what motivates them to cooperate.

**Compassion: The Great Mitigation**  Few people live in the extremes, except perhaps rabid left- or right-wing talk show hosts, and they are more product than person. Unless you live in a bubble, you experience the fact that people are affected by all of these styles. The more exposure you have to these different types, the more likely you are to be moved around, most likely toward center. It is easy in business, however, to get caught up in departmental wars and sectional tribalism.

The fact is, without understanding the impact we have on one another, we cannot have compassion; we move more toward a corner of the matrix. So, for instance, I am a selfish individualist at heart primarily because I believe it is the best way to improve the world—the underlying logic being that people work harder on their own ideas. Nevertheless, I have enough compassion to believe there must be a floor for those who stumble, get a late start, or simply give it their all and can't reach the bar. On the other hand, one of my closest friends is also a selfish individualist and he disagrees. He believes if you fall and can't get up on your own, then you should remain on the ground. Whereas my exposure to different types has moved me toward the center, his exposure has hardened his resolve to stay in the corner.

The more compassionate HELP MEs understand that giving takes resources from the person who is offering and that it as a kindness, not an obligation. Whether in business or society, you always catch more flies with honey than with vinegar.

**Dealing with the Opposites**   At first glance you might think the extreme opposites of the HELP MEs and LET ME HELPs are complementary, but that is true only when they are not polarized to the extreme. The needy, acidic you-owe-me type rarely gets assistance from the let-me-help-you type. Think back to the people in the story at my old company. The LET ME HELPs are much more likely to participate when asked for a hand rather than when told they owe it to help. When they are at extremes, they are no different from HELP YOURSELFs and YOU WILL HELPs and will end up at loggerheads in discussion.

**Mistaken Identity**   Sometimes people will convince others or even themselves that their core personality fits into one of the other buckets. The selfish collectivist can easily masquerade as the altruistic individualist because there is only a thin dime's difference between the two. Only by looking for motivation can you properly categorize and get to the real motivation for his behavior. If I put a face on one versus the other, I'd classify Al Gore as a selfish collectivist and Angelina Jolie as an altruistic individualist. Once you uncover the individual's real driver, you can motivate him in ways even he likely doesn't understand. In Al's case, you give him a Noble Prize and he feels motivated to continue his crusade to save the planet from cow farts. In Angelina's case, you let her adopt a child from a war-torn country and she gets her reward. (She doesn't even have a publicist.)

Now when you watch Al and Angelina in action in your office, you won't get them or their motivators confused.

**Conversion**  It's possible to go so far that you become what you hate.

The more extreme you become in a given category, the more likely you are to move to the opposite side or at least support it. While an altruistic person can slide into selfish territory easily, the cowboy needs real order to maintain that cowboy persona. He can find himself supporting the YOU WILL HELPs to maintain his help-yourself attitude. And while the YOU WILL HELP is busy forcing others, he can easily slip into the selfish individualistic model.

Once you understand the disposition of a person, you need to understand how he will take action to create an effective management style for dealing with him.

## *Action Matrix*

Instead of focusing on dispositions, now turn your attention to action styles as a way of categorizing people. The matrices are complementary; one does not replace the other. The disposition matrix is an important tool in creating a team and understanding how ideological conflicts will arise and where the areas are complementary. This one spotlights what actions a given person is likely to take based on personality traits. The result is meant primarily to predict outcomes and mitigate reactions.

Using the action matrix, you can create effective teams that are focused on your intended outcomes.

On the $x$-axis sits Impatient versus Enduring; on the $y$-axis, it's Positive versus Negative (see Figure 1.6).

**Impatient versus Enduring**  Once again, at first glance most people will want to identify with the trait that is considered a virtue. Since there's an old saying, "Patience is a virtue," by

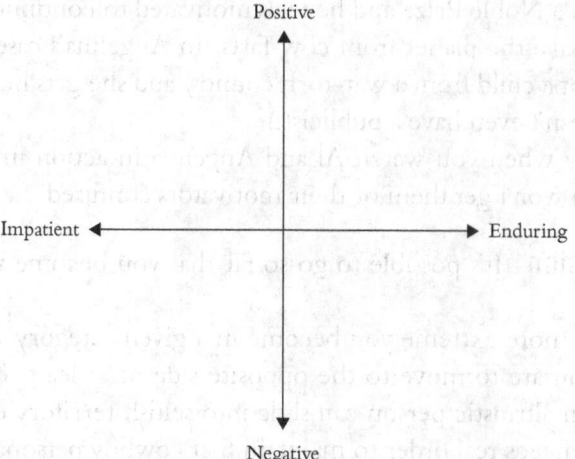

FIGURE 1.6  The vertical axis is about energy level in a direction. The horizontal axis is about degrees in handling time.

extrapolation our entire culture has condemned impatience to the opposite station, that is, a vice.

The two traits reflect a fundamental understanding of priorities: whether you get what you want when you want it or whether good things are worth waiting for. What happens when things don't turn out as hoped for? The long-suffering endurer can become quite volatile when, after waiting patiently all year, Santa brings her the wrong toy. Or after praying really, really hard for a month, you don't get promoted to general manager so you quit in a huff. So do not mistake enduring with tolerating nondelivery. One is simply willing to wait for what she gets and the other wants it on her own schedule.

Impatient people can be born that way and rewarded to maintain the trait or taught to expect their demands by you or others around them. Impatience itself is no vice if the expectations are realistic; they help people stick close to plans and a timetable. This is what I call *professional impatience*—establishing expectations and enforcing them. This is decidedly different from the two-year-old being allowed to dictate the family's behavior and schedule through screaming. This archetypal image illustrates a fundamental trait of impatient people: They see rules as a hindrance.

Regardless of the role a person plays in an organization, lack of respect for agreement can be destructive in both directions. On the healthy side, Eddie-the-Team-Leader sets scope and timeline expectations and then takes punitive measures when those milestones are missed. He drives action and creates operational excellence. On the unhealthy side, he is a tyrant ranting about your incompetence when you don't meet his unspoken expectations for what and when. Left unchecked or rewarded, he can become a cancer in your organization that makes people feel disheartened. The team concludes, "Nothing is good enough, so why bother?"

Enduring personalities likewise can have their roots in both nature and nurture. Essentially, this is a person who understands what is possible and wants you to deliver as promised, even though it may take awhile. Enduring can mean he is waiting for a promotion or an improvement on a widget. At any rate, he believes "good things come to those who wait," "patience is a virtue," and so on. He uses the system to get what he wants and rules are tools.

When well balanced, he can drive performance through setting expectations that are tolerant and reasonable. The patience may end abruptly, however, if you fail to meet the long-range timeline, whether for his personal goals or professional ones. The healthy enduring type can become an ambassador for common sense in midlevel management and inspired common sense in upper management.

Enduring people are good at mentoring and bringing others into an organization, assuming they bring the other traits you are looking for. Once in an intelligence job, an older gentleman said to me, "I think I know a thing or two. I have been here much longer than you have." The consensus of our group was he was worthless, so my answer to him was, "So has the furniture." If I'd had to deal with him long term and he decided to come after me, it is highly likely he would win because his patience for outcome is so protracted.

On the unhealthy side, some enduring people became that way because they are prone to inaction and don't mind the same in others. These are people who can't prioritize and have no sense of urgency. They believe that longevity is the key to success, and in some businesses, that's true. When the unhealthy enduring rise to the top through longevity, it is likely because the culture of inaction has led the other types to flee.

**Crossing the Line** Whereas selfishness and altruism are so closely tied they can become the other, this is seldom true of impatience and endurance. The shift here is tied to hope. An impatient person can be so driven by something she wants—like revenge—that she is willing to wait to get it.

First, action can be driven by the great human motivator: passion. The person who typically is impatient may turn to patience as she works her plan, putting all of the pieces into a master plan that takes time. Second, long-suffering people can go around the bend. They've had enough and explode in what seems to be an impatient response to a situation, or they move to the other side of the spectrum after they feel they have wasted time reaching for the desired result and lose hope. The breaking point of the enduring marks the point at which she becomes an impatient. Regardless of whether the action is patient or enduring, actions are tied tightly to the type of energy expended by the person. A positive enduring versus a negative enduring will have a very different style of behavior and ways of getting things accomplished (see Figure 1.7).

**Positive versus Negative** In this discussion, positive and negative energy are not a New Age look at the world. They are ways to describe where you apply the energy, not how much. Any given person is going to supply $x/y$ amount of energy on a topic, where

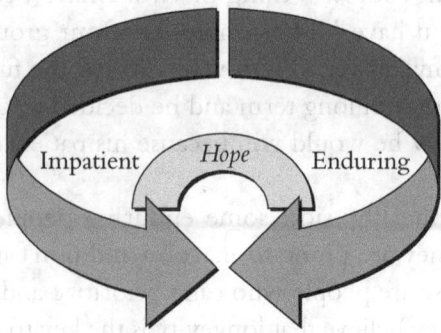

**FIGURE 1.7** The critical factor in where you remain on the continuum, or which direction you go next, is hope.

$x$ is total energy output and $y$ is total available. How he applies this is important. A high-energy person who applies little energy but tells you how passionate she is about the issue telegraphs information she is not aware of. The low-energy guy who gets wound up about his stapler missing, and yet says everything is okay, sends another message. A person's set point determines how much energy he will use and whether the inclination is toward positive or negative. You can have a cheerleader in the positive or negative sense. One is not necessarily bad and the other good.

In my early days in business as a construction project manager, these two extremes existed at one customer's site. One was an older southern lady, conservative in her speech and slower moving, but with a negative outlook. The other lady was slightly younger with high energy and more of a positive set point than the other woman. When something went wrong, the younger energetic woman would exert a fair amount of energy, but she toned it down at the suggestion of helping. The message was negative, but the energy to resolve the issue, clearly positive. Regardless, she did not come across as a happy person who wanted to be engaged in a problematic project. The older lady would declare with all the energy she could summon, "It don't work, it never worked, and it's never gonna work!" All of her energy was involved in criticizing, and while she was reveling in her negative glory, she seemed to be at her happiest. That was the time to co-opt her to get her objections on the table and prepare my plan of attack. Once you overcome the big guns, handling the bottle rockets is easy.

## Positive versus Negative: Focus on Positive

Positive-energy people are the eternal optimists, starting conversations with phrases like "what if?" and "there has to be a way." They see all actions as building toward their objectives instead of blowing up something to force a rebirth. They have faith in the existing system.

If they are high energy, they can become the cheerleaders of your organization, constantly attempting to get people on board for solutions and making everyone feel as if the unimaginable is possible. Positive people typically think the old way simply needs improvement. The positive high-energy person gives it her all and applies every bit of that energy to the cause she believes in for the purpose of building rather than destroying. When you don't see that level of energy, it's a sign she doesn't have passion for the topic. She sees value in continuous building and improving.

The low-energy positive can be the great unsung hero constantly rescuing others, but in a quiet fashion. When competent, she is seen as the backbone of the company with substance over flash.

Even the positive-energy types can be disenchanted like the younger of the two women at the construction site I mentioned; the result is they simply disengage. When this happens, you are likely to get negative responses from her as she slides over on the continuum. A positive converted to negative has lost faith and is not a pretty sight.

**Positive versus Negative: Focus on Negative** Negative energy doesn't mean the person intends negative outcomes. He simply sees applying negative energy as a way to accomplish a positive outcome. He has no faith in the existing system. His approach: Destroy the old or point out how bad it is and people will join you in building something better.

Negative-energy people bask in the fact you don't know what you are doing and take every opportunity to point it out. If they are competent in the area, they show you where you made your mistake; if not, they simply point out what you did wrong and that you should be better at it.

When they are high-energy and healthy, they are engines of improvement. They can create an environment of dissatisfaction with status quo and drive an organization to look for better things at every turn. But they still need the positives to help build it.

When high-energy and unhealthy impulses combine, that negative energy and cheerleading can lead to disagreement. For an organization, that can be toxic. All negativity with no solutions makes for a dismal work environment.

**Icon versus Artifact** The subtitle for this section should be, "Do any of these things fit together?"

Much of a human's perception is tied to ratios of gray matter to white matter, which is a topic I introduced earlier in this chapter in the discussion of what makes a good profiler. Although you cannot see the white matter–to–gray matter ratio of a person without written authorization and some pretty expensive tools, there are

behavioral symptoms that can allow you a good guess. More important, accurately pegging someone as predominately one or the other
has great value in predicting the actions that person will take. By
this I do not mean exactly what the person will do, but rather the
likelihood of action being taken and the intensity of the action.

### Icon versus Artifact: Focus on Artifact

Dr. Temple Grandin, a
very high-functioning autistic and professor of animal science, has
noted in her writings that the very high gray matter autistics see
everything in "pictures" or as a single concept when they are
learning and experiencing the world. I have spent a fair amount of
time watching horses on the farms and even conducted experi-
ments to see what they understand. What I find is that horses understand every artifact associated with food as food. There is no
chain of events or cause and effect. A horse will revisit a bucket he
has stood beside for hours repeatedly with nothing changing. He
also recognizes the feed room door opening means food, and my
going to the barn means food. Any other interpretation is simply
the human mind looking for cognition like ours in livestock.

I started to pay attention to people and see how much of that
thinking was apparent. In the beginning, I was surprised to find
people who were not far removed. On the extreme end are people
with conditions like autism and Asperger syndrome who cannot
link the absolutes of facts or faces to the underlying meaning. I call
this kind of thinking artifact thinking.

Artifact thinkers see concise, packaged information in every
concept or conversation. To say they take information at face value
would be a misnomer because many artifact thinkers analyze data;
they simply do not see the connections between one thing and
another. Revisit the example earlier in the chapter of the man
who built the well in the village: It never occurred to him that
constructing the well could be a bad thing.

Extreme artifact thinkers are great repositories of "how things
got to this point" and "who played what part." They can separate
facts from reasons, but application of the facts presents a challenge
for them.

More centered artifact thinkers, with enough understanding of
connections to keep the schedule together, make great executors for
projects or installation of new systems. They can see the task at hand,

cut it into component parts, and drive it to completion without stress about what might break downstream. Where they have difficulty is in the design arena. They cannot manage design alone, but clearly can contribute the factual details about what needs to be done.

### Icon versus Artifact: Focus on Icon    On the other extreme, there are the people who can take any set of artifacts or objects and create a story line for how they tie together. I use the term "icon thinkers" to describe these people. To people of various religions, icons integral to their worship represent morality and stories of struggle and triumph. Any given icon could represent an entire religious story, complete with the character development, struggle/plot, and finale. More important, these icons carry spiritual significance and a lesson. In days gone by, icons may have been the only tie certain people had to the "word of God." Interestingly, in Islam, images of people and creations of Allah are forbidden, a fact that has led to a great dependence on recitation and memorization by those who could not read. As a corollary, the Arabic language is one of the most iconic in the world.

By now, you are no doubt accustomed to my premise that traits taken to the extreme move into the territory of the polar opposite. This is true of artifact versus icon as well.

Go too far in the icon direction, and you start to see concepts as holistic ideas with no real tie-in to daily life. If you see connections between just about everything around you, you are, in effect, living in a world of your own creation. It describes not only conspiracy theorists who have gone well past reason but also some people in our society whom we hail as eccentric geniuses. It's the theoretical physicist who spends every waking minute trying to prove a theory once started down that road, giving no thought to trying to disprove it.

Icon thinkers find relationships and build the story behind every action or function they encounter. They seek to understand the connections between things. Icon thinkers *will* find the reason something occurred.

On the healthy side, they are great researchers who discover fantastic correlations, create cutting-edge theories, and solve problems for business.

On the unhealthy side they are people who find conspiracies behind the weather. They find correlations where none exist. In areas where data are not available to make a decision, conjecture can substitute. The danger in a group is that the bright, high-minded icon thinker posits a theory and the less-than-stellar thinkers in the group revere her for her genius. The next thing you know, her theory (fully intended to be theory by the icon thinker) becomes fact.

**Icon versus Artifact: Focus on Decisions and Action** Often, really iconic thinkers see the complexities of a situation as cause for analysis before taking action, to the point of so-called analysis paralysis. Alternatively, they may simply opt not to move ahead because the issue is so complex that any action might make the situation worse.

On the other extreme are the rash artifact thinkers. With wholly compartmentalized ideas, the artifact thinker will boldly take action. A lot of young people end up in jail because of this mentality blended with high levels of passion.

Passion of any type, whether revenge or something much more complex, will drive even the most iconic thinker to action. Passion will often override judgment, taking the individual out of the thinking or rational brain and into the reactionary or mammalian brain.

The iconic thinker with little passion to goad him can appear at the very center of the matrix. Even though he has very strong opinions, with so much thought invested in relationships between things but not much emotional energy, he is resigned to be an observer.

Imagine the signers of the Declaration of Independence—wealthy and educated, balancing decisions. Imagine the discussions about the unforeseeable consequences of establishing "inalienable rights." Take a few minutes to think about where each of these men would fit on the actions matrix, and then add the passion and fervor that overrode their original impulses. That will give you a reasonable model for looking at your organization.

## *The Categories of Action Styles*

This matrix of actions styles uses some terms that might at first look political until you take into account the meaning of each. They are people who

- Try to work through the system
- Tend to work against the system
- Want to blow up the system
- Aim to force overhaul of the system

Each of these types brings something to the table, and each of them in balance can ensure positive outcomes. But if you overload your organization with one style or the other, you should be aware of it and *make a conscious move to change the face of your organization.*

Remember, this does not replace the disposition matrix. It is compounding and simply the way a given person will take action.

**Legislators**   Figure 1.8 suggests that legislators, in the way I use the term here, fall in the positive-energy arena. For purposes of putting the concept to work in your business, "legislator" refers to a person who uses positive energy to work though a known system and endures to a desired outcome.

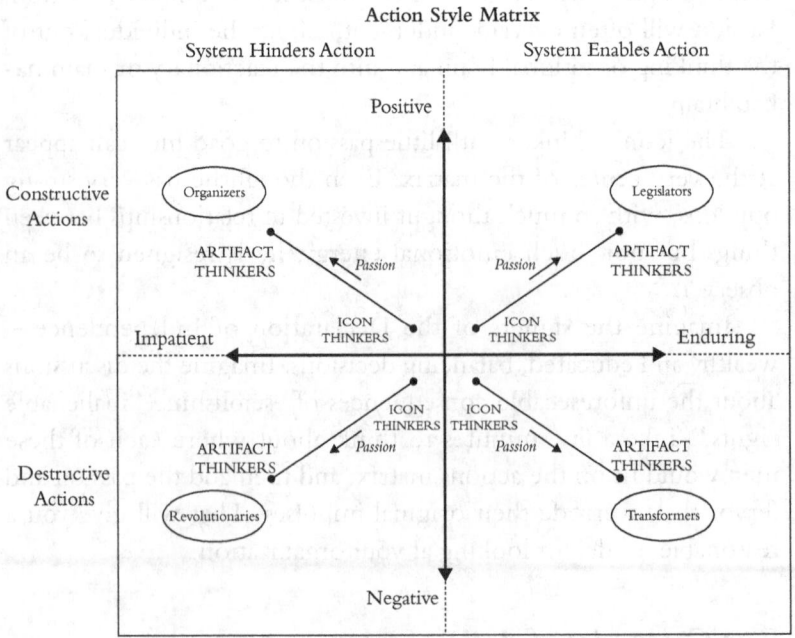

**FIGURE 1.8**   Legislator, revolutionary, organizer, or transformer: What is your relationship to the system and how much/how fast do you want to change it . . . if at all?

This is not to imply that some of the legislators in our modern world are not negative in energy and given to fits of passion with no understanding of cause and effect. This has nothing to do with disposition; you can find anyone deciding to work through the system to get what they want. This also has nothing to do with their intent; simply following the rules doesn't imply love of fellow humans or concern for coworkers.

Legislators bring stability to organization and create process for business.

When they are in balance, they allow the organization to get the basic blocking and tackling down to an art form, so it's easier to discover new opportunities.

When they go to an extreme, they create a byzantine labyrinth impossible for all but their own kind to navigate. They are the first to use the rules against you when you try to overcome their cause, and when it comes to revenge, the trap will be baited well and in plain sight.

**Revolutionaries** Revolutionaries have no patience when it comes to change; they want it now and see the entire status quo as the issue. We may have gotten here working through the system, but what makes us think we can improve matters using that same old system?

Revolutionary behavior can be targeted at the micro or macro level. Depending on their disposition, revolutionaries might be looking out for self or for others closest to them. They simply find fault in the system, and the opportunity exists to make it right—right now. They often know something needs to be done, but lack the endurance or patience to work though the system: "Let's just blow the whole thing up and make it work the right way!" If they succeed, they will want to blow that new thing up, too, at some point.

When in balance, they keep an organization nimble and looking to the future. They prevent the growth of convoluted organizational structures and allow for new ideas to crop up and rise to the top.

When they go to an extreme, they create a culture of upheaval and nothing gets done.

*Revolutionaries are best when balanced with the legislators to* keep things moving. When pushed into a role as a legislator, revolutionaries can be restless and agitating. If forced to implement, they will become true believers in their own process and often act more like legislators than revolutionaries.

**Organizers** Organizers see value in the system and believe in positive action to accomplish a goal within that framework, but they cannot understand why it takes so long. They see power to do more in numbers, and to that end, they create a group strategy to get things done. This does not necessarily mean their acts are selfless; they will simply build coalitions to get the project moving faster.

In society, people like this create actions such as Mothers Against Drunk Driving (MADD) and other social movements that prod legislators into action. Basically, they see things as moving too slowly, so let's add momentum.

This kind of mind-set can create odd dynamics in an organization as normally opposing dispositions join forces to move things along faster. Disparate types may agree that they cannot make things work through usual channels, so they combine to force action for positive change. They may speed up the process, but with disregard for the clashing motivations for the change.

In balance, organizers keep people focused so that they remember why they started the endeavor in the first place. They goad the legislators to quicker action.

Out of balance, they set the company's priorities as their own by constantly foisting their own ideas on everyone.

**Transformers** Transformers are like revolutionaries in that they see the current system as needing overhaul, but they take a much more patient approach to getting what they want. Instead of throwing out the baby with the bath water, they prefer to heat the water until the baby jumps out. They apply negative energy to remove slowly the pieces of the current situation they dislike, leaving behind only the things they do like. All along the way, they are likely substituting their own ideals so that in the end, the organization or system becomes exactly what they desire and only the outward appearance is the same.

If the U.S. Congress had term limits in place, we would see a lot fewer transformers on Capitol Hill.

In balance, transformers can keep the organization thinking and challenging its performance. They deliver fantastic results in transforming teams and business units when their ideas are aligned with the good of the business.

When they are not in balance, transformers become underminers. They are effective long-term planners who overcome objection by using the system.

**Commonalities and Catalysts**  *Legislators and organizers* believe the system has value and simply needs to be improved. The big difference is their level of patience.

Legislators can become disenchanted with the process and become organizers if they wait too long or if the prize they have waited for turns out to be a failure but they still maintain their positive energy. In terms American philosopher and social observer Eric Hoffer used, this is when the actual falls short of expectation and hope is lost.

*Revolutionaries and transformers* believe that the system is flawed and needs to be replaced. Again, the big difference is their level of patience.

Likewise, transformers can turn revolutionary if they wait too long or if the prize they have waited for turns out to be a failure.

*Transformers and legislators* believe a system is the answer and, by working though rules, they can accomplish their goals. The big difference is whether the system as it exists is good or bad.

They differ on whether the current system is worthwhile, even though both gravitate toward using the rules to accomplish their goals. Legislators see the system as valuable but needing improvement, which they are more than willing to do. Transformers see it as broken and useless but work through the system to replace it. When positive action does not work, legislators can easily become transformers as they lose trust in the system.

*Revolutionaries and organizers* both see rules as a hindrance or restriction in accomplishing their goals. They differ on whether the system is worthless and should be destroyed or whether it should be gamed to accomplish what they want. Organizers see the system as valuable but slow, so they create a pressing call for faster action to improve what they believe needs to be done.

Revolutionaries see the system as flawed and work outside the system to accomplish their goals.

If organizers are spurred to action by passion and see no reward from the system, they can easily lose trust and become revolutionaries.

*Revolutionaries and legislators* may be the same person, but at different times. Revolutionaries who set out to rebuild can become legislators and work through the system they create.

**Predicting Actions**  Combine drives—the HELP categories—with the types of people I've talked about so far and you can make some accurate predictions about how they will behave in an organization.

**First, a look at the HELP MEs:**
- HELP ME legislators

    Example: Al Gore, prior to his loss in the presidential election of 2000

    The action will be driven by creating a system that better serves his individual needs. The real drivers are the good he is doing for self and, as a corollary, how he can effectively use the system to get it. He has a sense of entitlement to what he wants and is willing to work tirelessly through the system to secure that entitlement. After he lost the presidential election and no longer had the opportunity to work this way, he turned into an organizer.
- HELP ME organizers

    Example: Candice Lightner (founder of MADD); Al Gore after he lost the election of 2000

    The HELP MEs organizers wield real power as they gather mass support for the cause.

    They understand that others must be feeling the same way, and they take advantage of it. Along the way, others get the same benefit—but that is not the driver. They want what they want right now and see the group as the means to get it. They align the arrows of motivation.

    On a small scale, this is the waitress who is underperforming but gets her friends to join into the tip pooling scheme. Or the seller of a product line who is failing but gets others in the group to create bundled selling opportunities. She can easily organize others of her own kind (the HELP MEs) and YOU WILL HELPs to drive her cause. When she chooses the right cause, she can engage the LET ME HELPs and the HELP YOUR-SELFs by drawing them closer to the human side of the issue.

Think about average Americans responding to collective efforts to rebuild New Orleans after Hurricane Katrina or to assist Haitians after their devastating earthquake. All but the staunchest opponents of collectivism were swayed by calls of compassion.

The same can be true in the business world when a person feels wronged or cheated and creates a coalition to change the rules. This is about gaining entitlement through mass movement and gaming the system through the use of the rules.

- HELP ME revolutionaries

Example: Fidel Castro (before he got a job as dictator)

The HELP ME revolutionary looks for opportunities to overcome what he sees as a stagnant system blocking his progress.

People given to get-rich-quick schemes fit this category. I've seen many people with this profile jump into multilevel-marketing.

In an office setting, a HELP ME revolutionary will want to destroy the status quo to rebuild it around "how the world works now," which is code for "what we have isn't working for me." He is not above helping others in the process as long as he gains benefit.

- HELP ME transformers

Example: Madalyn Murray O'Hair, who removed prayer from public schools

HELP ME transformers whittle away at the system's rules that offend them to create a system designed around their desired outcomes. They use the rules against the system.

**Next, a look at the HELP YOURSELFs:**
- HELP YOURSELF legislators

Example: Karl Rove

A HELP YOURSELF legislator will look out for his own interests, all the while working within the system.

They take on roles in corporate America to ensure that there is minimal intrusion to local offices or champion changes to policies they see as restrictive. In the political world, they work to make regulations less restrictive and protect individuals' rights and incomes. They are against social programs and against programs that make anyone aid someone else. The neocons (that is, the current generation of right-wing politicians) fit this bill; they believe that larger government is designed to protect individual rights.

- HELP YOURSELF organizers

    Example: "Tea Partiers"

    This type does not believe the system is broken enough to throw out, but is unhappy with how slowly the changes occur. The modus operandi is to game the system by overwhelming it. The organizer in this case is looking to take back control of the system. In the office, she builds coalitions of like-minded folks to present grievances and get what she wants; once she gets it, she'll probably slink quietly back into her old status.

- HELP YOURSELF revolutionaries

    Example: Thomas Jefferson (pre-presidency)

    This person sees the system as so onerous and limiting that it must be worked around or destroyed.

    On the low end, the revolutionary works simply through passive resistance to the rules. On the high end, he goes to war with the offending rules and completely disposes of them.

- HELP YOURSELF transformers

    Example: Ayn Rand, novelist and philosopher known for the system called objectivism

    This person is a cowboy focusing all of his energy on dismantling the controls of the system.

    In an office, this person goads the sales team into thinking "every man for himself," because he sees the advantages of a hotly competitive structure superior to teaming.

**The third set to examine is the combinations involving LET ME HELPs:**

- LET ME HELP legislators

    Example: Andrew Carnegie

    The LET ME HELP legislators, above all else, want to choose whom to help and when. They work through the system to become major contributors to the good of others, but they will use that understanding of the system at any opportunity to stop mandates for help. Working through an established system to help, Andrew Carnegie offered $20 million to the Philippines to buy their independence from the United States; $20 million is the price the United States paid Spain for the Philippines.

- LET ME HELP organizers

  Example: Bill Gates

  LET ME HELP organizers lead with their own energy and resources to create a movement so that others can contribute.

  They are keenly aware of what they have to offer and provide that as a catalyst for getting things done. The overall intent is to get others to support a cause they believe in. In an office, this is the cheerleader for fixing problems, and perhaps getting everyone to kick in to help someone facing a problem. On a grander scale, it is a philanthropist leading the way with her money, intent on having others support the initiative.

- LET ME HELP revolutionaries

  Example: Ross Perot

  LET ME HELP revolutionaries will invest all of their mental, emotional, and financial resources to promote their cause.

  Rules don't matter because their commitment and belief in cause supersede everything. In the office, they give time to the project they see as valuable, even at the expense of other supposed priorities. But when forced to work on a project against their will, they refuse and create a disturbance about how "busy they are" with more important matters.

- LET ME HELP transformers

  Example: Ronald Reagan

  These types of transformers want to spend their resources to help others; they look for ways to reduce obstacles so that you can help them effect a renovation.

  They take negative actions to dismantle the system, which they don't think works all that well. Along the way, they introduce more rules, but they are the "right" rules. In the office, they are the ones who don't want to do away with rules; rather, they want to adjust them to become more reasonable, more reflective of common sense. An example of this type of action is when Ronald Reagan dismantled social programs believing that nonprofits would fill the gaps.

**And finally, there is the set of YOU WILL HELP characters:**
- YOU WILL HELP legislators

    Example: Nancy Pelosi, first female Speaker of the U.S. House of Representatives

    YOU WILL HELP legislators understand collective thinking and the application of rules to reach their objectives. They drive with fervor to create more rules as they build the system that will be best for all concerned. In business, these architects often miss the mark by not asking the users what they want.
- YOU WILL HELP organizers

    Examples: Mahatma Gandhi and Martin Luther King, Jr.

    YOU WILL HELP organizers use the overwhelming support of the group to get to a greater good.

    Typically, they see the system as well intentioned, but flawed and in need of improvement. Driving for change, they follow their belief that many voices are better than one. In the office, they create coalitions to get rules changed. YOU WILL HELP organizers are the classic union organizers.
- YOU WILL HELP revolutionaries

    Example: Vladimir Ilyich Lenin, leader of the Bolsheviks

    YOU WILL HELP revolutionaries drive fervor in pointing out that the system is broken and that all stand to gain from its replacement.

    Whether it is your compensation strategy or the assigned parking policy you just implemented, YOU WILL HELP revolutionaries look out for the good of the group and are not afraid to blow things up to get it.
- YOU WILL HELP transformers

    Example: Harvey Milk, first openly gay man to be elected to office in California

    Looking out for the good of the group, YOU WILL HELP transformers dismantle the pieces of the system they oppose and replace it with rules they see as better.

    These transformers are driven by outcomes for everyone, and it can often become a point of ego. They will move ahead with a new and better system by using the rules against the system. In the office, they are the ones who find the loopholes.

As you think about the people in your organization, give yourself permission to create tags for each of these categories or use the examples. And remember: Someone who is Ayn Rand today can become Thomas Jefferson when her patience runs out.

## Profile Your People

With these summaries in mind, plot your team, office, or company on the chart.

Is your organization a legislator frozen in inaction by the complexities of the system, or a revolutionary organization with the passion to get things done? Or something else?

Get the profile right, for your people and your organization, and you can not only predict actions but also change what individuals and teams will do.

Here is the most important profiling question for you as a business professional: Now that you have a new understanding of personal dispositions and action strategies, do you think your organization is properly aligned? That is, do you have the balance of types in your company and on your team to succeed? Or did you stack too many of one type and miss the mark?

You can change the action styles of people, but it will be stressful. If the action styles do not match your needs, you must decide: Is it worth all of that stress, or do you replace the people?

CHAPTER 2

# Question Like a Polygrapher

## Tools
- Reading of body language
- Use of body language
- Questioning styles
- Questioning strategy
- Deception detection

A polygrapher is an interrogator armed with a sensitive instrument. Information is obtained through the use of this complex tool and good interrogation soft skills. The electronic device allows the polygrapher to establish a baseline on three axes and then look for deviation. To achieve the desired outcomes, the polygrapher (1) says and does things to affect the person's emotional state and (2) questions with intent.

The outcomes: The person divulges information of value, some of which may not be obvious at first, and reveals his or her personality and facts through deviation from baseline.

A polygrapher does not just ask straightforward questions to get information. Pieces are strategically put into play to secure intelligence about the person, a situation, or thing.

Although one of the tools polygraphers use (the actual machine) is neither available nor practical for you to use, the others are; namely, good questioning and reading a *baseline,* the way a person behaves and speaks normally. You can establish a baseline easily by reading behavioral cues just as reliably as polygraphers do when armed with their lie detectors.

Interrogators overwhelm their subjects with psychological ploys to the point where they "break" and start to talk; they then use their body language and questioning tools to ascertain whether or not the subjects are lying. Polygraphers use ploys, too, but simply to elicit responses allowing them to know whether or not someone is hiding information. I refer to a combination of those two skills sets in this chapter because, in business, you will rarely have the opportunity or motivation to use heavy-handed interrogation ploys to soften the person before you start the discussion. Instead, you aim to create an environment in which the person wants to talk and then use body language tools, questioning style, and deception-detection techniques to get exactly what you are after. This chapter is mostly about straightforward styles of information gathering with little discussion of manipulation. But don't be disappointed: I'll get to manipulation later in the book.

## Value to Business

You want to question like a polygrapher when you want the truth and you do not think you're hearing it. Using the skills in this chapter will help you investigate a problem, get information, and do discovery related to a project or a customer's need. More important, once you know how to use this skill set, it transfers to other areas of your business. So although you might not need to know whether someone is lying, the same skill applies in daily conversations that could result in conflict. For example, in a situation involving terms and conditions of an agreement, these body language and questioning skills will enable you to learn what the customer really needs, what his or her sensitivities are, and how far you can push. You want to be able to detect when the person is receiving your message or when that person is merely nodding and saying yes, without really understanding.

The following two scenarios describe real problems at companies I've worked with. At the end of the chapter, I will take you through the kind of questioning that resolved them.

## Scenario 1: Investigate a Problem

A tragedy occurred during a routine equipment installation: The installer fell off a roof and died. Five people witnessed the accident. I had done a lot of training for the company the man worked for, so the staff had been sensitized to the fact that questioning is a special skill.

In a situation like this, every person believes he or she is telling the truth about the incident. What happens in reality is that people hear your question and, whether it's on a conscious or subconscious level, evaluate what you are trying to get from them. They consider what's at stake for them. After that, they proceed to answer the question. At that point, they either filter the information or give it to you the way they remember it.

The company sent someone who knew the task at hand:

1. Manage the emotional state of the witnesses to ensure that they would be as rational as possible in responding to questions.
2. Avoid seeding questions with ideas that could influence the response.
3. Identify main styles of deception.
4. Understand the impact of emotion on details.

She also needed to customize questions along the way as she listened to the witnesses' answers.

That's the way to get statements that withstand scrutiny. The company was not at fault for the employee's death and the accounts made that clear.

## Scenario 2: Discovery Related to a Customer's Need

Mel represented his company in talking terms and conditions for an equipment installation that, from his customer's perspective, were exceedingly rigid. Mel had to talk through a set of inflexible provisions that reflected a risk-averse mentality with an executive at a property management firm; he had a corporate mandate to take risks. In fact, the company had established market dominance because of its risk-taking ethos. What it came down to is that Mel spoke a language that his customer did not relate to. Mel's challenge was to make the sale despite the sharp differences in point of view.

In some ways, it's what an investigator for the Environmental Protection Agency (EPA) might face in relating to the Amish farmers over their cultivation techniques. The Amish farmers consider themselves stewards of the land and farm in a way that uses as few resources as possible. From the EPA's perspective, implementing that philosophy causes environmental destruction. What are the chances they will learn to speak the same language?

In Mel's case, forging an understanding was an achievable goal as long as he used questions to uncover his customer's hot spots and guide his thinking. Primarily, he had to use them to reinforce a bond of trust. Any good salesperson will tell you that people don't buy products; they buy relationships. The customer will continue to spend money if the relationship is on solid ground.

In behaving like a good polygrapher, Mel had to get the customer to relax and to trust him; he had to ensure the customer did not feel as though he were under pressure. At the same time, he had to ratchet up tension a bit, so he could see how the person acted under stress.

## Theater of Polygraph

What's your image of a polygraph experience? You see someone sitting near the lie detector machine and suspect Central Casting sent an actor with steely eyes and no laugh lines. You are hooked up to the machine, with tubes across your upper chest and abdomen, metal plates on the ring and index finger, and a blood pressure cuff around your upper arm.

The polygraph instrument collects physiological data, measures it, and records the results. It's designed simply to alert the polygrapher that something about you has changed in relation to a given stimulus. As the polygrapher asks you questions about something that should give you cause to be concerned, he or she is focused on whether or not you show concern. The polygrapher also asks questions that should not arouse any stress; if they do, that, theoretically, also tells the interviewer something about your concerns.

The polygraph experience originally wasn't intended to cause stress the way it commonly does today. However, people who used lie detectors quickly realized that the theater of them was as powerful as the measurement. The intimidation factor can accelerate the process of getting results if the person hooked up to the sensors perceives the machine as being able to perform voodoo magic. It can also impede the process.

A good polygrapher relies on knowledge of human behavior and a fine-tuned ability to devise and pose questions to obtain information. This is exactly what an interrogator does, but the polygrapher learns to apply questions while using technology. A bad polygrapher relies solely on technology. This is problematic because when the machine causes stress, it becomes a prop in the drama of questioning and can reduce the polygrapher's ability to obtain valid responses during the exchange. The real art of a polygrapher is not sitting there and staring at a machine.

In business, there is a corollary: You live and work in an environment filled with scary settings and theatrics. The core lesson in this is to use those tools to create stress when needed, but not to rely on them.

## Tools of Questioning

Many of the soft skills described here support the same functions as a polygraph—but they are far more portable. From good questioning and knowing how humans interpret intent to following the flow of a conversation, these skills can deliver accurate readings.

You were born with the body language abilities I describe here. Many developmental studies show humans are designed to read faces from infancy, for example. Our upbringing blunts these abilities. Time to turn them back on.

At some point, you were the world's most annoying questioner once you learned which questions were the easy ones and which were the difficult ones. Any parent can remember the day her child learned the power of "why." In this case, I want to arm you with a more effective set of questions to get your information. You can still use "why" when you need to annoy someone, though. I'll also give you a couple of tools that will help you get at the truth when you are certain someone is lying and you want them to know that you know.

## Reading Body Language

I've written an entire book about reading body language, so don't expect this section to give you a comprehensive knowledge of reading people. This is a crash course aimed at giving you succinct guidance on reading body language in a business environment. It's strictly for the purposes of detecting stress and determining in a basic way how someone feels in relation to you: connected or repelled, subservient or superior.

**The Big Four**   Humans have four big categories of body language in common: adaptors, barriers, illustrators, and regulators. They can look different from person to person, but they always serve the same function in communicating.

• Adaptors

Adaptors are movements to release nervous energy. They are the rubbing and petting gestures, the twitches and glitches that occur when you feel uncomfortable. Everyone has some version of an adaptor; it may show up frequently or perhaps only when the person is under high stress. Adaptors enable you to focus energy in one place; that can give you a sense of feeling in control.

There is no single type of action that constitutes an adaptor. Just about anything can become an adaptor. When you know a person's baseline, you can determine whether or not a particular movement is an adaptor, as well as the intensity of stress causing it. Increases or decreases in adaptor use mean the person is having a control issue; you need to discover why.

### Exercise

Step 1:  Discover your own adaptors.
Step 2:  Identify other people's adaptors.

To become familiar with your own adaptors, go someplace where you feel you don't belong or will be noticed as new. For example, if you're Jewish, go to Mass at a Catholic Church. If you're a man, hang out at a women's shoe store. If you're 50, dig your old board out of the closet and go to a skate park.

(On second thought, maybe find something less injurious. I like my readers. Maybe try dropping in at a store where these guys hang out.)

To learn about other people's adaptors, go to a municipal office and watch people coming in to apply for permits and pay tickets. If you are part of a large company with a human resources department, observe people coming in to apply for a job; take a look at their mannerisms as they sit and wait to be called. Even in ordinary meetings, you will see adaptors as people who are unaccustomed to speaking are called on to contribute information.

- Barriers

Unless you have a trusting connection with a person, you will protect your space. The way you do that is with a barrier, which can be the way your use your body or an object. You have no doubt heard the expression "giving him the cold shoulder"; that movement of turning and putting your shoulder between your face and the other person is a barrier. A desk, purse, arm on a table, lid of a laptop computer—all of these serve as barriers. You can use it deliberately to give yourself more space, or you can fall into the habit of sitting behind a desk or computer and not even realize that you have disrupted the connection between you and the other person. On some level, he senses it. An increase in the use of barriers means the topic or situation makes the person uncomfortable.

### Exercise

Gauge the effect of barriers.

In a few one-on-one situations, such as a meeting with someone you barely know or a conversation with a stranger at a cocktail party, remove a barrier in the course of talking with the person. For example, if you are sitting behind a desk, start with items like papers and a coffee mug between you and the person. During the conversation, move them aside and find a

*(continued)*

(*continued*)

reason to invite the person to share the desk. For example, slide your laptop over to the side so you can both view the screen. Pay attention to any differences in the way the person acts.

Now do the converse. During the conversation, use barriers to increase your space and establish more separation. Observe and listen for changes in demeanor that signal a shift in comfort level. Think about how you and others in your office have your workspace set up. Does it foster openness or say, "Stay away"?

- Illustrators

Illustrators punctuate your statements. You might hammer a point in for your audience by striking your fist on the podium. When you want to make someone feel welcome, you don't just say, "Come in"; you probably extend your arm to illustrate your sincerity.

Illustrators are a natural part of communication, used by people regardless of physical constraints. They take different forms depending on the person's culture and physical makeup, but they are there. On one occasion, Maryann had a deaf student in her audience at a presentation at a university. She noticed that the interpreter using sign language emphasized certain words and phrases by putting more power into them with her hands. The way she did it seemed to correspond to Maryann's shifts in volume and use of illustrators. Illustrators are the mind punctuating the message. Wrong illustrator = conflicting messages.

### Exercise

Talk without using illustrators.

Decide before you have a conversation with someone that you will not use any movements to emphasize what you're saying. That includes eyebrows, feet, and every other part of you. Your cadence, pitch, and tone will still illustrate, but not your body.

See how long it takes for the person you're talking with to say, "Are you okay?" or to simply act perceptibly weird in response to you. Even if you use illustrators only conservatively, the other person will notice that something is different.

### Exercise

Watch for mismatched illustrators.

The best place to see illustrators that do not match up with what the person is saying is in the U.S. Capitol. When members of Congress give speeches about legislation they don't know all that much about—but are supposed to care about—their mouths say one thing and their arms convey something else. Look for incongruity like this at conferences and seminars when someone is giving a presentation and during speeches of candidates for public office. When people think they are supposed to be gesturing, as opposed to gesturing naturally, it's a sign that something is amiss. Either the person is nervous and has practiced movements believed to be appropriate or the person is being disingenuous.

- Regulators

You use regulators to manage another person's speech. Sometimes, they are obvious movements such as using your hand like a stop sign. Often, they take a more subtle form because you want the person to stop talking or speed it up, but you don't want to be rude. You might tap your foot on the floor or a pen on the table, or you may take a step back to suggest you're leaving. They are all regulators.

### Exercise

Notice how others use regulators.

Set up a conversation at work that involves at least three people. Of the group, one person should be a talkative person—one of

(*continued*)

(*continued*)

the chatty people who answers a simple question with five paragraphs—and one person should be someone who seems to always be in a hurry or prefers to hear himself or herself talk. Ask a few questions that get the chatty person wound up and watch how the other person responds. If the hurried person just walks away, try it again with someone who's more concerned about being rude.

**Baseline**    People generally fall into one of two schools of thought regarding body language: the absolutist and the baseliner. The absolutist believes that a scratch of the nose means someone is lying. Baseliners look for what is normal when the person is speaking while relaxed and responding to questions normally, and then watch for behavioral symptoms to change. The symptoms obviously aren't a definite indicator that the person is lying; rather, they indicate that something has changed, usually as a result of stress or at the very least new inputs.

Once you see the symptoms change, then you pinpoint the reason by using other tools.

There are three main places to look for deviation in baseline:

- Voice
- Word choice
- Body language

**Voice**    The voice is highly subject to the effects of fight or flight, which is a state of stress described next. Vocal chords clamp or tighten under stress, creating a change in pitch. When you hear this effect, pay close attention. The person's tone of voice is a good indicator of change. We all know the phrase, "It's not what you said; it's *how* you said it."

Few of us pay attention to pitch and stridency. It's also common to miss the significance of someone stressing words. They receive emphasis because the brain finds them important; listen for these indicators of real thought. I also pay close attention to changes in cadence of speech. If a person normally rattles along and suddenly starts to speak in a halting fashion or slows down, it indicates that the brain has shifted gears. The person may be navigating uncharted territory. When the voice speeds up, it can indicate energy about the topic or a desire to move away from the one just finished. Listen for volume changes, too; these can be a signal of a person's emphasis or desire not to be heard. Ask yourself what might have prompted the change.

**Word Choice** When a person uses a word that seems out of place for his vocabulary, pay close attention. It indicates that the tidbit may have been prepared ahead of time. The person may be apprehensive and arming himself for the issue or may simply be trying to expand vocabulary. You discover the reason based on further scrutiny.

An odd word choice can also suggest that the person is trying too hard to fit in. When a man from New Jersey says "y'all" to folks he's just met in a bar in Huntsville, Alabama, it might be a sign he feels out of place.

**Body Language** All people have a natural energy level and style. This includes their own personal choice of adaptors, barriers, illustrators, and regulators and the frequency with which they use them. Any deviation from normal for people—using adaptors more or less than usual, hiding or showing more of themselves than normal, using the hands more than usual or not at all while speaking—are important indicators that something has changed in their heads. Again, you need to look for the reason behind the change.

**Baseline: The Holistic Look** Think of these three categories—voice, word choice, and body language—as parts of speech. You can listen to any one piece and read absolute meaning into it, or you can coordinate your perceptions to get the entire picture. Consider the HELP ME revolutionary, exemplified by Fidel Castro before he became a dictator. When you ask this type of person what the genesis of his latest idea is, for example, and you see his adaptors increase, it might be simple discomfort with the environment rather than tension related to what he is saying. But when he crosses his hand in front of his crotch and taps his toe, you have a reliable indicator of stress and you need to dig to understand why it surfaced.

Keep the concept of baselining in mind as you read through the rest of the chapters in this book, realizing that anything can be "normal" for a given person. What you want to know is the difference between normal and anything else.

**Fight or Flight**   Before delving into questioning styles, it's important that you know the symptoms of fight or flight, which is a decided deviation from normal. Questioning can arouse this response, as extreme as it is. In fact, you've likely seen it without even recognizing the symptoms. To better equip yourself to recognize these systems, you should know what they feel like. When you know the early symptoms, you can short-cycle the fight-or-flight response.

---

### Exercise

Purpose: Vivid recall of fight or flight.

**Nonbusiness:**
A ferocious dog ran directly toward you.
You were held up at gunpoint.
A police officer stopped you for speeding and you had been
   drinking.

**Business:**
You made a horrible mistake in a meeting; the boss seethed
   with anger.
Your presentation to a group of key executives imploded.
The president of your company appeared at your door
   moments after you blew a major deal.

---

When you see someone in a state of fight or flight, you are dealing with a person who has strong emotions and is physiologically ready for action. Consider the preceding situations that apply to you and how your memory of those moments affects your reactions, even years later. If you've been stopped by a cop, the sight of flashing lights in your rearview mirror may trigger slight trembling. A traumatic experience giving a speech will cause your heart to race when you see a podium. These are signs of fight or flight.

The human nervous system has sympathetic and parasympathetic components. The sympathetic system revs you up for fight or flight, and the parasympathetic system throttles you back to a state of resting and relaxing.

Within milliseconds of a shock, the sympathetic system responds to the perceived threat by putting the cortisol cycle in motion; that means stress hormones pour into your system. There are a number of bodily actions that you control voluntarily, but in that sliver of time, your body takes complete charge. It turns some systems on and some systems off so that you have blood flow and energy where you need it. Some changes occur instantaneously—and are the signs that mean your mind is at war:

- Blood travels to the muscles.
- Blood travels away from the face and skin, as well as away from the digestive and reproductive systems.
- Muscles receive an extra dose of glucose from the liver to prepare for physical activity.
- Cognitive functions become secondary to basic animal functions; for example, you're better prepared for running a mile than doing an algebra problem.
- Heart action speeds up to pump blood to all the right places quickly.
- Breathing rate increases in response to the heart pushing glucose through the systems; this pumps oxygen to the muscles.
- Metabolism accelerates, so the body starts sweating.
- Pupils dilate to collect information about the perceived threat.

The results of these changes are external and internal. Inside, you may feel jittery, and because of the reduced blood to your digestive system, you may get butterflies or a sick feeling in your stomach. You feel your heart race. Because blood is leaving the skin, you get the feeling of an elevated temperature and cool skin at the same time; that is, you feel clammy. And even though your rate of breathing has picked up, tightness in your chest causes the feeling you aren't getting enough oxygen. Your concentration on the threat intensifies; you want to see and hear everything relevant to your safety. Emotions come to the forefront, which is why many people cry when they are frightened or angry. Don't mistake the tears for a sign of weakness.

You can see the external symptoms of fight or flight; the intensity will vary:

- Complexion appears pale, or actually, paler than normal, because the blood flows away from the skin. This affects people of all skin color; with light-skinned people, the effect is just more obvious.
- Lips appear thinner than normal; as part of the digestive system, less blood is sent to the lips and mouth in this state.
- The lower eyelids droop, again because of blood moving to the muscles and away from the face.
- The chest begins pounding because of the rapid heartbeat. The shoulders may rise and fall as breathing speeds up.
- Hands shake as a result of increased metabolism.
- Nostrils flare and breathing becomes audible as the body struggles to take in more oxygen.
- The eyes either squint or become wide, depending on how the person instinctively tries to take in more information.
- The brow may be clinched and drawn downward, indicating anger, or it may be high and eyes wide open, indicating terror.
- Shoulders rise up, elbows go closer to the ribs, and hands close up into fists—posture indicating defense or escape.
- Sweating occurs as the body tries to cool down in its hyper state. This type of sweating involves massive amounts of by-products, producing noticeable body odor.
- In really extreme situations, the person ultimately collapses.

You can also hear the sound of fight or flight: The voice sounds higher in this state because the vocal chords constrict and the mucous membranes become dry.

If some of these signs sound too extreme to ever occur in a work environment, think again. Even if you've never felt threatened in a meeting, watch someone who does feel threatened. A common scenario is someone speaking to people in higher positions, having to defend against a harsh challenge to something he or she just said. Maybe you won't see a fist, but it's highly likely you will see shoulders rise, elbows draw in, and one hand clutch a laser pointer with full force. Many of the other signs of fight or flight will be there, too. You just have to look and listen for them. When you do, you will see the threatened person lick the lips, struggle for breath, and clinch the brow and you'll hear an increase in the pitch of his or her voice, among other signs.

## Using Body Language

Usually, people with exposure to information about body language know something about understanding it. You've only just begun with that information. The complementary power is knowing how to use it to your advantage.

### Countering Fight or Flight
You need to make sure you aren't a victim of fight or flight.

To some extent, the ability to have control relates to ego states. Do you have a collegial relationship with the person, or is it more parent-child, where one person has power and influence and the other person is deferential due to youth and/or inexperience?

After an April 27, 2010, Senate hearing grilling Goldman Sachs executives, I provided some commentary to Bloomberg on Lloyd Blankfein, the chief executive officer and chairman of Goldman Sachs. The producer asked me to help them create a report card on his performance and that of the other people on the Goldman Sachs team who testified.

One piece of body language I highlighted occurred when Blankfein was watching Senator Carl Levin, chairman of the Permanent Subcommittee on Investigations. Blankfein's face projected absolute contempt. Regardless of his words, Blankfein's tone of voice and expressions showed he was incredulous at the business ignorance of someone in Levin's position. He did not feel a need to be deferential to his "polygrapher."

I gave him a "B" because the face-wrenching made him unbelievable to Americans. My exact words in the April 28 interview were: "No matter whether he's being honest with his body language or not, that is not something that makes the American public like him."

At the same time, I saw those extreme movements as natural for him, as part of his baseline when he is displeased. I concluded he probably made the same kind of expression in his normal office setting; he sees no need to be deferential to anyone. On that point, I said, "If you were an employee of Mr. Blankfein and you saw that look, you would not be happy with what was coming out of his mouth afterwards. He's holding back contempt for the person he's talking to in lack of belief that the person can't understand what he's saying. It's very clear."

So, the same expression in two different circumstances. Same emotion, two different meanings. He might have a very different baseline when he's displeased with his family or the people he does charity work with. Same face, and a related emotion, but a desire to project something different because of his emotional connection to the individuals.

I noticed something else that takes us to a discussion of emulating the alpha, that is, the person to whom others give deference. When Levin questioned Dan Sparks, former head of Goldman Sachs' mortgage department, he squinted his right eye—and that's exactly what Blankfein often did as part of his expression of contempt. I have to wonder how many times Sparks had seen that and just subconsciously integrated it into his own repertoire of facial moves. Something or someone would trigger the "I'm displeased" response, and the eye would press shut.

Michael Swenson, who was a director in the structured-products group, earned an "F." He was a soup sandwich. If I were a coconspirator, I would hate for him to be captured first. He leaked toxic levels of emotion.

Most people would probably gravitate toward Swenson's response because testifying before a U.S. Senate committee would be a rare and threatening experience—much like taking a polygraph.

How do you remain more like Blankfein than Swenson? Prepare. Fight or flight happens typically because we lose control of our faculties. Many effective countermeasures exist.

One really ugly side effect of fight or flight: It turns off "useless" things such as cognitive thought, because fight or flight is all about preparing the body for survival. By doing a little contingency planning, you can prevent yourself from slipping out of cognitive thought and into an emotional pit. It's like trekking up a glacier, losing your footing, and then doing a quick self-arrest by sinking your ice axe into the surface. Educating yourself to recognize the signs of fight or flight equips you with an ice axe. It means you can engage the frontal lobe and talk yourself out of panic. If that isn't enough, here are just a few additional tools you can use.

**Physical Activities** Develop a set of activities such as curling your toes in your shoes. Not only is the act a superadaptor that will release high amounts of nervous energy, but it also takes conscious thought to do this and will recenter you. You can hide anxiety while you collect your thoughts. Opera singers use this technique because it allows the vocal chords to function properly while the singer channels nervous energy; one awful alternative would be a strident voice.

**Preamble Phrases** Many high-level executives use this one, whether inadvertently or by intent. Keep some phrases in your mental first-aid kit that lead into any kind of material. A lot of people learn to use them to avoid saying "um" or to help control stuttering. They are phrases such as "There is so much to consider" "What do you see as the facts here?" and "To the best of my understanding." They are rehearsed spacers. They do nothing more than allow you a moment to collect your thoughts before you get into the fire. Interrogators and investigators use this frequently to give them seconds to think of the next question. People who do a lot of interviews on talk shows, especially call-in shows, often rely on them to keep the flow going while they think of a substantive answer.

**Learned Response** If you are the kind of person who needs a bag full of tools designed specifically for one function, then do some contingency planning. Practice expected outcomes. Think about worst-case scenarios. In fact, think of everything on the spectrum between worst case and undesirable. If you take this approach, you will have conditioned yourself in advance to deal with an emotionally disruptive issue. When the actual issue arises, more likely than not, you will be prepared and energized for action rather than afraid. There is a complementary discussion on this point in the chapter on decision making.

**Face the Tiger** Although no one in his or her right mind fights tigers in a business suit, facing a surrogate tiger can teach you how to be prepared for the worst. Find a surrogate for the issue you will have to deal with—a noble foe who can step into the role of adversary in full makeup and costume. If you are afraid that September's board meeting will be brutal, find someone with the knowledge and personality to play the role of a challenger. Another approach is to find something equally disturbing, such as speaking to a local Rotary group, to prepare for the fight so that you won't go into fight-or-flight mode.

Continue the list with your own options, keeping in mind that the tools are based on three factors:

1. Preparation
2. Desensitization
3. Engagement of the thinking brain

Now that you know what stress looks like in yourself and in others, you are ready to get down to business—without falling apart under stress. Are you going to respond like the four-year-old who just asks, "Why?" "Why is this happening to me?" or "Why are you doing this to me?" Or, are you going to respond like the exasperated parent: "The answer is 'because.' Now suck it up and figure out how to deal with it."

I guarantee you will see stress eventually. Once you can control your own response to it, you will be in an excellent position to learn how to turn the tables so you detect others' stress and can take advantage of it.

In the following sections, you will learn how it feels to have that control, either from the beginning or after you have countered an attack. You will see how to question masterfully to discover true feelings and uncover deception. The first step: understand basic questioning styles and strategies.

## Questioning Styles

Style is often built around purpose. You may have multiple needs for asking questions:

- Obtaining information
- Determining a baseline
- Causing stress
- Redirecting the conversation

During questioning, you have to understand how people think and guide them in delivering the information you want in a manner you can use. This is why questioning styles are so critical, and why you need to match your questions to the people, not just the situation. In other words, you will draw heavily from the lessons of Chapter 1 on sorting personality styles. A key idea to carry over, for example, is that detail-oriented questions about *why* someone did something are likely to arouse a stress response from an altruist who focuses on the big picture. ("How dare you ask, 'Why did I try to save the whales by ramming my boat into the ship at high noon?' ") If that's the kind of response you want, then go for it. On the other hand, if collecting intelligence is your driver, you should try a different plan.

Another factor is how much time you have for the exchange. If you have very limited time, you have to plant questions that people will want to come back to you later to answer or you need to create an *anchor point*. As you move through the questioning styles, the examples and exercises will illustrate how to do that.

Polygraphers always need a baseline for their subjects, and so do you. For a polygrapher, baseline questions might be "What's your name?" and "Where do you live?"

After that, the questioner might want to raise your stress—to see what physiological reactions you have when you're lying. The polygrapher could simply say, "Tell me a lie," or ask you a question that shocks, such as, "Have you ever had sex with your sister?" In questioning like a polygrapher, you will also ask questions to evoke stress deliberately.

Interrogators learn there are good and bad questions. Military interrogators are taught six types of good questions; I have found that even the so-called bad questions have value if used deliberately. Asking a question that's too complex for someone to answer easily must be a tactic, though, not a mistake. So let's take a look at each of these question types so that we can then pull them into a strategy.

The types of questions generally considered "good" are:

1. Direct
2. Follow-up
3. Nontopic

4. Repeat
5. Control
6. Prepared/canned

Good questions require a narrative response. They give people a chance to talk, which gives you the opportunity to observe their eye and body movements and note changes in tone of voice, cadence, word patterning, and pitch. Using a yes or no question has value if you want to lead someone in a particular direction with your questioning, but it gives you almost nothing to go on in terms of body language.

**Good Questions** Let's take a closer look at the six types of "good" questions:

- Direct questions—simple, clear, focused on getting the facts
  - Example: "What are you doing here?"
- Follow-up questions—hooked onto a response to the previous question
  - Example: You asked a colleague how yesterday's planning meeting went. She responds that nobody seemed prepared. You ask, "What piece of it were you supposed to prepare?"

In U.S. society, it's within the bounds of politeness to ask about anything that a person has introduced to a conversation. In inter-rogation, we call these *source leads*. So if a woman you've just met at a conference says, "My aunt just died a horrible death," that's an opening to ask for the details on the death, despite the fact you just met her. That kind of statement is an invitation to talk about the subject. On first blush it might seem rude, but I can guarantee you leads are in the conversation for a reason. People want to bleed information on the subject they brought up; I call it a mind bleed. Watch for changes in body language that indicate a need to back off.

- Nontopic questions—casual, off-topic
  - Example: Early in a sales call, you ask about a photo on the prospect's desk, "What a beautiful boat—have you sailed a lot?"

Military interrogators learn the term "nonpertinent questions" to describe these questions, and they have been considered valuable only in building rapport. I have long disagreed with that assertion. I think all questions are pertinent. Anything that elicits a response from you allows me to see how you think, what the mechanics of your brain are.

If a person is insecure in a role or repeatedly returns to that role as part of a pattern, then that uncertainty in the current role or venturing into new roles may leak out in answering what appears to be a nontopic question. For example, let's say you are new to a managerial position and I ask you how your softball game was last night. The insecurity you have about your management capabilities might show up in the way you talk about your sterling performance in the game. You want to convey to me that you know what you're doing—at least on the ball field. The transference of competence will probably come out in the same way transference of character comes out when the person accused of murder points out he is a church deacon.

Nontopic questions can also break a person's concentration. If you think someone is lying to you, you can use it to interrupt the flow—he won't remember where he stopped, which gives you the opportunity to take the conversation in another direction. Then you can revisit the subject and see how the information differs.

- Repeat questions—the same thing asked in a different way
  - Example:

Q: "How was your day on Tuesday?"
  A: "Fine. I went to Wal-Mart."
Q: "I hear they have puppies now. Did you see any?"
  A: "Yeah, I saw some cute ones."
Q: "Do you think they still have them?"
  A: They usually have them for four or five days.
Q: "And how long ago was that?"

The conversation turns to the kind of puppies. The questioner then comes back to Wal-Mart. The intent is to verify the activity and timeline, so by asking the question in components, you are asking the same question again while masking it in a new topic.

Polygraphers use repeat questions a lot. It lets their source know they are on to something and allows them to drill down. Keep that in mind as you practice using this type of question. A repeat question is not redundant; it's another door into the same house.

When you become aware that someone is deliberately using repeat questions, the tendency is to resent the style of questioning and get emotional. Ann is an acquaintance who did customer training for a computer company that primarily served the federal market. She had a security clearance and could work at intelligence and defense agencies, but she knew her income would jump if she earned a higher clearance. She applied for a job working directly for a defense agency. During her polygraph, the questioner asked her if she drank alcohol. "No," she replied. A little later, the questioning turned to her friends and social life. "Do any of your friends drink alcohol?" She told him and then he asked, "Do you ever join them?" Again, she said, "No." At another point, he explored her past and asked simply, "Have you ever had a problem with alcohol?" Ann got furious. "I told you I don't drink!" The point of the repeat question, of course, had nothing to do with whether or not Ann drank. The questioner used the tactic to see how emotional she would become and, if she did show stress, how she would cope with it.

The best way to handle it in any context is to remain aware of the game that's being played and stay dispassionate. You want to compartmentalize, to keep your psyche separate from the issue.

- Control questions—questions that elicit nonstressful honest answers

    In interrogation, this is a question to which the subject knows the answer. It could be about chemical weapons if that's the person's area of expertise, or it could be about the terrain in her home town. In business, I have found that the best control question is simply a question the person has no reason to lie about.
    - Example: "What was your high school mascot?"

Typically, the only reason I ask control questions is to get a baseline. Because the person has no reason to lie in response (theoretically, anyway), you can perceive how she behaves when no threat is present. I inserted the parenthetical because, if you're using this skill in an interview environment, you may think a simple question such as, "Where were you last employed?" constitutes a control question, but that may not be true. HR Solutions, a Chicago-based management consulting firm, did an extensive survey about employee retention and found out that one out of every twenty-five employees quits on the first day. If the person you are interviewing is one of those, how likely is it that she would admit where she was last employed? So a classic control question is better, perhaps one that asks about how the person applied for the job. It taps into memory and gives you a solid answer.

- Prepared questions/canned questions—based on research into the topic the subject is being questioned about

  When the topic is complex and you need to configure the questions carefully as opposed to structuring them on the fly, you want to use questions that reflect research. Questions like this would have been particularly useful to senators questioning Lloyd Blankfein—someone who is not tolerant of people who don't understand his business. In the interrogation world, canned questions are useful when the topic is technical and you want to appear knowledgeable. It allows the interrogator to build rapport and get information relatively quickly.

  ■ Example: You're meeting with a customer in the property management business, and you want to discuss professional services. You prepare a list of questions in jargon he would use to describe his biggest opportunities to make money and factors that affect his bottom line. It allows you to speak his language instead of asking him to educate you or speak your language.

Prepared questions make the person asking the question look smart about a subject. They can help you take a story apart relatively quickly because you appear to know what you're talking about. The person may be less likely to stray into exaggeration or any other kind of deceit.

As I said before, one of the hallmarks of questioning like a polygrapher is questioning with intent. Asking a question designed to show off your knowledge in a particular area forces someone to delve into his area of expertise.

Once you know the sky is blue you can ask, "Why?"

Let's turn now to the questions generally considered "bad."

**Bad Questions**   These five types of questions are based on lessons taught to interrogators day in and day out. These questions are bad only when you don't know how to use them intelligently. All of them can have enormous value in redirect and to establish a baseline.

- Yes or no questions
- Leading questions—This can be a yes or no question; the questioner projects an answer. If you find yourself asking "to be" questions, then you are asking leading questions. That is, if you are asking "Is your wife a genuine blonde?" or "Are you really a vegetarian," then you are posing a question in which you are likely projecting an answer.
  - Example: "Did your daddy's connections get you promoted in the company?" The response is almost guaranteed to be no.

You can often use leading questions to change the direction of the conversation. The use of this question can drive the source into a tirade or rant. He would suddenly rise up about how underappreciated he is for his real talent and tell you his father's shadow isn't large enough to take the sun off his face. The answer delivers heavy source leads around relationship, emotional state, and personal beliefs, all of which are open to discussion. I don't consider that a bad question at all.

Because leading questions can help you cut through posturing and evasive language in so many situations, I want to illustrate its use in a real scenario. As part of my work for a manufacturing company, I attended a meeting with one of their vendors that was seriously underperforming. Representatives of my client company caused stress by their very presence. The vendor representatives knew they had failed, so they had a deviation from baseline just walking into the room.

In a practical sense, then, the people we met with weren't real.

If you aren't aware of the artificiality of that encounter, then it's very easy for everyone in the room to get caught up in the emotion inherent in it. Someone needs to be an outside observer with control over the environment—often a good role for a consultant.

In this meeting, the salesman from the vendor company started spouting metrics. His approach was clearly "If I dazzle them with numbers, maybe they won't notice how awful we are." If you're going to attempt that, you have to make sure that both parties have the same system of measurement; otherwise, you're just talking past the other guy, and annoying him in the process. It's like two guys sitting in a bar talking about how beautiful their girlfriends are. One of them describes his catch as a tall, skinny blonde. The other guy says, "That's too bad. A woman without curves is as pretty as a two-by-four."

I could tell the two sides were talking at odds, so I finally just threw out a leading question to the vendor: "Do you agree that you are shorter than last year?" A simple yes or no in that situation moves the conversation away from game playing and artificiality. Then the vendor becomes a participant in a conversation.

- Negative questions—These questions plant confusion.
  - Example: "Are you not going to the annual conference?"

The only time you use negative questions is when you want to create confusion, you want to drive the conversation, and you want to create misunderstanding. You create agitation with misunderstanding, so it becomes a tool to knock someone off balance. The reason interrogators are taught not to use negative questioning is precisely the reason you would. You want to create confusion and an opportunity for your subject to get rattled or ask for clarification. It is especially effective in tag teaming. That request puts one questioner into the role of providing solutions and allows the other to get more information about how the person thinks.

- Compound questions—These have more than one answer.
  - Example: "Did you take the highway and then stop at the customer's office or take the frontage road and end up at the office after you had lunch?"

These are not good for a lie detector test where you want to know which part of a question caused negative energy to surface. The only good use of this type of question is to test how effectively someone can follow the logic of the questions.

- Vague questions—Multiple interpretations of these questions are possible; uncertain parties or actions are questioned.
  - Example: "Did you see them doing that?"

The Army taught us not to use vague questions in interrogation, but they became part of my skill set when I saw their power. They cause people to ask for clarification; when people do that, they bleed information. On a more complex, vague question, such as, "How do you think you would handle a tough personnel issue?" you have a couple of alternatives when someone comes back with, "What do you mean?" For example, you can say something equivalent to, "You decide." Allowing the person to interpret the question will probably cause a rise in anxiety. Or you can play with the vague question and, in the process, see how the individual's brain works.

A truly bad question is one that you ask like an interrogator trying to get raw facts through intimidation. For example, "Who were you with last night?" That kind of confrontational question is off-putting. If you learn to incorporate various types of queries into a robust conversation, then you can get the information you want without stabbing someone with a pointed question.

Another truly bad question is on the opposite end of the spectrum in terms of directness. Think about how often members of Congress are guilty of this. They deliver a five-minute statement to show off the fact they've done some homework on an issue, and then at the end, tack on a "Why?" No wonder witnesses often sit there glassy eyed and respond with canned answers.

Your question has to be clear enough to be understood and sufficiently part of the conversation so that it doesn't seem abrupt.

## Questioning Strategy

A polygrapher or investigator of any kind is going to start from a requirements document, which sets her objectives. If she is a police interrogator, the document might be simply a confession or it might be actionable intelligence. In the case of an intelligence officer, it might be information to target a person who can spy for the United States. In the case of a business executive, they most often fall into discovery of needs or into an investigation of an incident. Regardless of the case, the key elements are the same:

1. Nature of information
2. Timeline
3. Relationship
4. Sorting style

**Nature of Information** In a discovery session, you must begin the session understanding what you are looking for. That drives your questioning strategy. First, categorize information you want into usable buckets such as budget, timeline, and personnel. You might have a different strategy if your information objectives are company morale and future plans.

By ordering the information you are gathering, you can quickly assess a few things about the information and how to approach your subject.

- How sensitive the information is that you want to discuss
- How important the issue is to you and the source
- Your level of understanding of the issue

**Sensitivity of Information** The relative sensitivity of the information—how freely you can talk about it—will drive your choice of how much rapport building and nontopic questioning you use as you probe for what you want. If it's submerged and difficult to get from your source, as a first step, you will want to use nontopic questions to open source leads. For example, if you suspect a morale problem has crept into the department since Joe was promoted, you might throw out a question such as, "What do you think of having Ellen, Ted, and Joe plan the company picnic again this year?" If you get a remark such as, "Joe's potato salad was horrible," you have an opening to discuss what other things Joe doesn't do particularly well. That is, after following the source lead, you can shift to good follow-up questions to get the rest of the information.

You should also consider that the person you are talking to is following an internal process while listening to you. The person hears your question, processes what you are asking for, interprets how that fits with personal needs, and then decides what to answer. Although the mental action is lightning fast in most cases, it always occurs, even if on a subconscious level. As you ask questions about sensitive information, watch the source's body language and notice changes. Among other things, increased use of barriers, shifts in posture, and increased use of adaptors can signal outright discomfort with the topic; continuing with that line of questioning might not be possible at that moment. Move to another topic and let the conversation flow. Once the conversation starts to become more fluid, you are likely to get more cooperation when you lightly probe again.

**Importance to Source**   Knowing how important the information is to the source will help you understand whether your arrows align. The alternative is having to ask a lot of less pertinent questions. If that's the case, not only do you need to be keenly aware and prepare questions to prevent the source from feeling alienated, but you also need to weigh the subject's concerns and yours closely. If the person feels traumatized because of Joe's promotion and you think you can solve the problem by simply moving his office down the hall, you have a mismatch on the gravity of the morale problem. More important, if you have little interest, the conversation can drag and never get to your real interest, which in this case, might have to do with pulling the team together for an important new project. If you want to be manipulative, based on the nature of your relationship, you might toy with the source by teasing with questions about lack of interest and then moving the person off the project. Be careful, though. Whereas in intelligence work, this kind of negative approach often brings people back to you with fervor, in business, this kind of manipulation tends to backfire. You will see more of how this works in Chapter 5 on negotiation.

In the intelligence world, young collectors are a danger not just to the enemy but also to our national security. By design, an interrogator or investigator knows where the holes in our intelligence picture are. He is there to collect information around that intelligence gap. The problem occurs when he becomes so impassioned about the information that he runs headlong into a line of questioning that allows the enemy to reverse engineer: If the intelligence guy tells the enemy how many things he doesn't know, the enemy will soon have an image of what he does know.

The intelligence world has a remedy for that problem—aside from firing the person. Analysts serving as collection managers feed requirements to the person who will be in contact with the enemy without letting the collector know what the real need is. If he fully meets those requirements, he will satisfy the needs of the intelligence community but not be in a position to reveal anything of value. Generally, however, the collector is aware of a bigger picture and will mask body language and balance the need to collect with what the source needs to hear to keep talking. The lesson for you: Keep the conversation flowing. Don't make every statement or question about what you need.

**Level of Understanding** In the intelligence world, collectors are often called on to ask highly technical questions of experts in complex fields. A prepared set of questions becomes vital in this situation. Often the person doing the questioning studies and makes detailed notes about the topics before gathering the collection requirements she will use. The setup could easily create a stilted encounter, so the intelligence professional must adopt role-specific behaviors to prevent that. Inexperienced collectors prey on the nature of human beings to teach—"As someone who studied nuclear physics, I find your theories intriguing"—while more seasoned collectors might take the role of simply being non-expert in an unrelated field who's a good listener. In either situation, if you are not expert in the field, you need to pay very close attention to the body language of your source to ensure you get the pieces that are important while balancing what you came for.

Timeline Polygrapher interviews are finite; the theater is the thing. The polygrapher is simply looking for areas of deception; detecting them may lead to later interviews. Police interrogations can wear on for hours, days, or even weeks in sessions. Intelligence interrogations work the same way. The primary reason for these long, drawn-out interrogation processes is that the source needs to "break" before discovery can begin. There is a fundamental difference between that threshold and what you aim for. Another fundamental difference is that most intelligence collectors and police interrogators do not need to work with their sources on a continuing basis, as you do. As a side effect of the short-term nature of the relationship, interrogators often run roughshod over people and see them as expendable. A glaring exception involves investigators of internal affairs. Many of them develop horrible reputations, and scores of movies have been built around the concept because they are in continuous contact with the very people they suspect of criminal activity. I point this out because, as you get adept at using these tools, you may feel compelled to get the information you need and become heavy-handed in the process. If you have an ongoing relationship with someone, take the sessions in stages if you don't need the information urgently. Use a phone call or e-mail to point the next discussion where you want it to go. In a situation where you do need the information promptly, create a sense of need that aligns the arrows to make the source want to talk about the same things you do. And if you are involved in a real investigation, of course, the theater of sounding like an interrogator might serve your needs best.

Relationship  A twenty-year professional relationship with a colleague is very different from a session with an irate customer. As such, they deserve very different approaches. The nature of the relationship dictates the relative need for rapport building and deference. The latter is often misunderstood because many people see deference as linked to rank. The fact is, people display deference in a situation because someone may have more expertise, is a better dresser, or has the power to terminate a contract.

Start the meat of the conversation after you have a grasp of the nature of the relationship. If there is any sense of a power imbalance, for example, that will affect how people respond.

I was just working with a company on a project that was of monumental importance to them. The company aimed to upgrade the way every one of their service personnel used technology to meet customer needs.

One afternoon the president of the company asked me how the project was going. "The ground truth is that it's stressful for the technicians, but it's going pretty well. The older guys don't like the thumb typing. Other than that, people are adapting to the change." And so he committed on the spot to going to the site where these technicians were headquartered and meeting with them personally. He wanted them to express their problems.

"Don't," I told him. "These guys will never come clean with you because they are under a lot of stress. Everything they tell you will be filtered by their fear. You are the president of the company. They can't talk to you comfortably."

He did not get it. He had brought me in to the project to make things happen. Part of that scenario was that he presumed people would be afraid of me because of my background as an interrogator. People at his level, according to him, were afraid of me.

But that wasn't true of the guys on this project. They were afraid of John, who seemed like the alpha gorilla—not someone who could understand their concerns, but someone who would order them to go away.

John did not understand the image he had because of his title, and how it profoundly affected how people perceived him—even without knowing him. Because he had worked his way up, he still thought of himself as one of the guys. He had to understand how others saw the relationship with him if he were going to be successful in getting honest answers from them.

**Sorting Style** You have natural ways of sorting facts and memories that affect how you interpret questions and statements. When demonstrating baselining, for example, I might ask a person to recall what her kitchen looks like so that the audience can see where her eyes move in retrieving a visual memory. Some people respond with, "It has blue and white walls with a hardwood floor," whereas other people will tell me the color scheme, what's in the flower vase on the table, and the make and model of every appliance. The people who talk in big picture terms are what I call large chunkers. The detail-oriented people are small chunkers.

People also have a tendency to separate in terms of sequence, time, and event. Sequence people have a strong sense of the relationship between things. Time-focused people will tell you a story that gives you a sense of hours and minutes. People who remember things in terms of events may not know what happened before or after the event, or what time of day it occurred, but they can tell you about the event itself.

Knowing something about a person's sorting style will give you great opportunities to spot deception—a time-focused person who has two hours "drop out" of a day raises suspicion—but it can also pose problems in questioning. If you ask for a report on a conference in terms of priority of events but the person tends to think in terms of sequence of events, you may not get the information you seek.

## Detecting Deception

People typically lie in one of four ways:

- Commission—completely fabricating a story or event
- Omission—leaving out the juicy bits
- Embellishment—exaggerating
- Transference—moving details from someone else's life into your story

Before seeing how you break the lie, you need to detect deception.

In most people, the mere act of lying creates stress. Psychopaths, who have no conscience and are not compelled to tell the truth, might show stress only when they fear being discovered. In either case, fear creates metabolic stress evident in the spectrum of fight-or-flight responses. Simply mentioning an issue that is sensitive can cause the cycle to start and the person to present symptoms. When the person first starts to feel the impact of fight or flight, like the polygraph, you can see "blips on the screen" in the form of a person's body language. These blips indicate that you should look closer to discern what is causing the stress.

### Body Language Signals of Stress
When someone experiences stress, the following responses occur:

- Blood flow to the nose increases. People often start to feel itchy around the nose or face and place a hand there to scratch or partially cover it. That indicates stress, but not necessarily deception.

- People touch their brows. Stress causes people to feel the need to massage the muscle between the eyes; it's the main muscle where Botox is injected.
- Use of adaptors such as stroking, petting, massaging, and wringing increase. These types of adaptors indicate that a person is feeling the need to take control of her environment.
- People find cover. Increased use of barriers indicates discomfort with the topic.
- Voice pitch changes. Vocal chords constrict, emphasizing the offending message.
- People look for the door. People in a situation they do not want to be in will look for the door figuratively by pointing to it with appendages like feet, or they may literally look for the door.

**The Microinterview** Any one of these bullets describes blips on the screen that make you know you need to dig deeper. When you need to dig deeply, the tool to use is a microinterview. You open up the offending area as you move along in conversation. As you observe changes in body language, note where they occurred. Was it around a specific timeline question? Or about who was at the party? Regardless of what the trigger was, you know it needs further discussion, so you delve in and focus the conversation on the issue until you find out what is causing the blip.

Here is how you would proceed if the blip occurred in relation to timeline:

I start a conversation about last Tuesday.

Q: "What did you do last Tuesday?" (I know he is an event thinker, so I need to work my way into a timeline.)
   A: "I went to Wal-Mart."
Q: "I hate going to Wal-Mart. The lines are always long. I know you do, too—what took you there?"
   A: "I needed a new printer cartridge immediately."
Q: "You must have been in a hurry. How long did that take you?"
   A: "I don't know. An hour or so." (At this point, I see stress appear.)

So now the conversation begins to be about what time of day and how crowded the store was at that time. I can easily dig deeper into the cause of the stress. He might be stressed because he ran into his ex-wife at the store, or he might be hiding something more serious. If he's using a lie of omission, that is, simply leaving out salient details in his story, as I get closer to the details, his stress will become more visible.

Q: "Wow, an hour is a long time considering the store is five minutes from your house. What took so long?"

A: "Well, I ran into an old girlfriend. We talked for a few minutes and then I went home." (I notice real stress related to the girlfriend, and then immediate relief in telling me he went home.)

As the conversation continues, strong indicators of deception surface as he uses words to jump over a time span. Instead of saying, "We talked for about 45 minutes and then I left," he leaves out a chunk of details. When I drill in, I see even more stress.

The microinterview is just as useful for discovering why someone is feeling stressed about an issue as it is for uncovering a lie, so don't blind yourself by projecting that it can root out only a lie. When you're a hammer, the world looks like a nail.

**Breaking a Lie**    Assuming you are in the position to force someone to tell the truth, the tools for breaking lies are straightforward.

* Commission—In the course of the conversation, note when stress arises. Ask for more details related to the issues that seemed to cause it. You are just tightening the noose. Typically, a person doesn't think through an entire lie, but rather focuses on the pieces that are important to him. You are coming at the information from a different perspective, though, so you can use that to your advantage in asking about details he hadn't thought about. Relating the story to the rest of his life also adds a level of complexity he probably won't be able to handle: "And when you spoke with Steve Jobs at Macworld, what did he say when he saw the apple tattoo on your forehead?"

- Omission—Use forward and backward passes at timelines. Few people are weird enough to practice their lies backward. Consider the saying, "He knew his subject forward and backward," which suggests the person has an intimate familiarity with it— the kind that would almost never be associated with a lie.
- Embellishment/transference—This combined category of lying is the hardest to break because it is based in a true story—just not necessarily your own or to the degree that you actually experienced something. In the case of someone else's story, ask for tie-in details to uncover where the seams of the lie meet the person's real life. They could be related to timeline, location, or other people who were involved, among other factors. In embellishment, ask for others who can corroborate or ask questions about the outcome. For example, "What did your friends do when you wrestled that bear? I'd really enjoy hearing what they were thinking!"

Armed with a suite of tools to question well and detect deception, let's now return to the scenarios presented in the early part of the chapter and see how they did play out, as well as how they could have played out.

## Revisiting the Scenarios

### *Scenario 1: Investigate a Problem*

Immediately after the incident, the lead investigator asked me, "What do I need to know in talking to the witnesses?"

The first thing I said was, "Do it now." Waiting a few days seems like the right thing to do because it's human nature to back off after people have experienced a trauma. The rationale is that they need to calm down before talking about it. That's absolutely wrong. Get the details right away.

The minute the witnesses get to a point of stabilization and normalization, they start to place blame and try to figure out why the incident occurred. They will read into the situation.

Immediately after an ordeal like this, people are in a state of displaced expectations. The brain has not had a chance to delete, distort, and generalize. The information from them will be raw and honest. That's not to say it will be 100 percent accurate, but it will be the unfiltered truth rather than synthesized explanations.

You do want to wait until a person is stabilized to ask a question such as, "How are you doing?"

In short, the person will be better able to assess his own state after some time has passed but will be better able to give you valid details of the incident immediately after it occurs.

For purposes of discussion, let's add a twist to the accident of the man falling off the roof. Pretend that one of the witnesses was on the ground just beneath the man who fell. A second before the tragedy, he yelled, "Stop!" in a threatening voice at some teenagers he saw tampering with his truck. The interviewer arrives on the scene and asks the man to describe what happened. He blurts out in a semi-hysterical state that he had just yelled at some teenagers and, even though his partner on the roof had never been bothered by noise before, maybe he lost his footing when he heard shouting. The man may well change his story later as he normalizes and realizes that his initial admission could make him culpable.

In questioning the witnesses on the scene, the interviewer has to avoid evoking emotion or confusing the witnesses. Nontopic questions, as well as the so-called bad questions, have no place here. She has to be sure the witnesses stay on topic and understand exactly what she is asking them.

## Scenario 2: Discovery Related to a Customer's Need

First and foremost, Mel does a little more research about the nature of the company he is dealing with and then goes to the legal department and gets the extent of the wiggle room in the terms and conditions. As he starts the conversation, he notices the terms and conditions bring up a response in the brow of his client. It's a body language signal of concern.

He says, "I know your company is founded on high risk, and it is a successful business model for you. We, however, are not as mature in taking risks as you are." Mel is playing to the strength of his client. He continues, "I will, however, see what I can do. What do you see as an acceptable threshold?" He wants to get the client to be the first to budge because the client might not ask for the full concession Mel knows is possible. When the client asks for less than Mel knows he can get, he says, "I think that's doable," and both are happy.

Polygraphers use tools to observe stress, and those tools are not portable. But they also use tools that are common to all investigators that are portable. These skills are good not only for questioning, but also for finding feelings and drives in everyday conversation.

Establish a norm for the person you're talking to and look for changes. After that, drill down using a microinterview to discover why things changed. You might find a lie, or more important, the truth.

CHAPTER 3

# Network Like a Spy

**Tools**
- Elicitation techniques
- Five questions
- Countering elicitation
- The fulfillment strategy
- Tools of influence

Given a choice, I prefer a direct and confrontational style. Occasionally, I use some tools of persuasion that you might call manipulation, but that style is neither acceptable nor usable by all people.

Outwitting someone is not evil. In contrast, manipulation and toying with someone for its own sake are not healthy. With those thoughts in mind, I offer you lessons from the darker side of the business. Even dark tools can be used for a good cause.

The National Clandestine Service (NCS) of the Central Intelligence Agency (CIA) sends officers to foreign countries to network. Through professional and social connections, they determine who would be helpful in securing intelligence. They then build trust with them, and eventually, recruit them as assets and agents. An asset facilitates covert operations by doing things such as passing messages to an agent or figuring out where to place a bug; an agent provides intelligence. After that, the focus is on maintaining those relationships. That last piece is the one that is most often overlooked.

Polish Colonel Ryszard Kuklinski provided critical information to the United States for nine years. Long after the officer who handled him was transferred, he continued to have contact with him through letters, and when that officer was no longer able to write the letters himself, the Agency wrote the letters in his name so that the bond between agent and officer would remain strong. To network like a spy, you must be prepared to invest in relationships for the long haul.

On its most essential level, networking like a spy is easy. I yawn; you yawn. The automatic mirroring response suggests that human beings are networkers on an organic level. With slightly more sophisticated moves, such as a tilt of the head and placement of hands, the same mirroring occurs when someone decides he wants to bond with you. Much of what you will learn in this chapter is how to exploit that natural human tendency to connect.

## Value to Business

You can use skills to network like a spy whether you aim to collect information or to create bonds—and effective relationships—with people for professional or personal reasons. You can establish a good spherical vision of how relationships really work and better maneuver around and between those relationships by using these tools.

In the spying game you often cannot turn the supreme commander to your side, but you can easily turn one of his subordinates to get the same effect. The key is to exploit this reality and build the right network, not necessarily the sexiest.

In building a network like a spy, you will target two categories of people: those you focus on for short-term intelligence efforts and those with whom you intend to cultivate a long-term relationship. In the first category, you might put contacts you meet at a trade show or conference who leak information of value. In the latter are people who will look out for your good and throw themselves on the tracks for you. You want to build your long-term network in a way that relates to your mission. That doesn't mean handing out business cards at a cocktail party and hoping the desirable people call you later.

Regardless of how long the person remains in your network, developing useful relationships is rarely a one-way street. Nor should it be. Typically, you deal with a quid pro quo: I give you something, and you give me something. The variables in both the world of espionage and business are similar. Maybe I give you money, access, or critical information; you give me something that you consider just as valuable. Maybe all I give you is hope. Maybe that's all you want. And maybe, unlike most real spies, you make a few friends along the way.

This exercise spotlights how networking like a spy will serve you well regardless of whether you're in sales, information technology (IT), accounting, or management of a fleet of trucks. In it, you are specifically not after the big fish, but rather someone who usually walks right in front of you and escapes your radar.

### Exercise

Connect with a "boring" person with the aim of having
   him or her offer to do a favor for you.

Choose someone in your company with whom you have no interest in forging a relationship; you've concluded that the person has nothing to say that will interest you. Start chatting. Make a concerted effort to be genuinely interested. Spend most of your time listening. Stay alert for information that indicates common interests.

Steer the conversation so that it's clear you have a particular need. It could be for certain information, a document, an introduction to someone, or a latte from the local coffee shop. You succeed in the exercise if you end the conversation with the person offering to either get, or help you get, what you need.

This exercise is a short one. The real test is doing this over the long term, and with someone who really matters in carrying out your master plan.

## The Brain of a Spy

In real life, "spy" refers to the enemy. She's the one who infiltrates your organization to discover secrets and set people up for a fall. And then she disappears without a trace. For our purposes here,

I'll use "spy" to describe anyone who engages in activities designed to collect actionable intelligence.

I chose the pronoun carefully because women tend to have a lot more innate abilities than men that make them good spies. That's because the fundamental activity of spies is recruitment, and to a great extent, that's largely a right-brained social activity that capitalizes on intuition, reading emotions, and projecting empathy.

A third-rail topic that people do not like to discuss is the difference between male and female brains, and it pertains to team building, project management, and other aspects of office life. It's fine to talk about the differences based on Myers-Briggs characteristics, for example, but as soon as I assert that men and women have complementary—not identical—brains, you'd think I had set off a stink bomb in the room.

People of both genders usually get offended when I say that women's brains tend to make them better at details, subtle communication, and intuitively reading other people. I didn't make this up. Not only have I observed it, but neuropsychiatrist Louann Brizendine also wrote an entire book about it, called *The Female Brain*. So feel free to take offense, but know that what I'm asserting is fact.

This is not to say that all women's brains are identical or that all men's brains are identical. I simply mean that we can use basic differences to round out the thinking on a team and to understand better what predisposes some people toward being good at networking.

## Form and Function

In a spy network, every person has a function. Take a lesson from that. That doesn't mean you don't have friends who are part of your networks. Naturally, people you know, love, and trust are de facto members of your network.

Now think beyond those people to contacts who have tremendous importance, or potential importance, to you. You may not love people in your professional network (in fact, don't), but you should know and trust them.

Good networking doesn't just happen any more than a good round of golf happens. It takes work, acumen, and a few steps:

- Design your network
- Recruit your people
- Motivate behavior
- Maintain your network

## Form

The guiding questions in networking fall into categories:

- Whom do you want?
- Why?
- How will you get to your short- and long-term targets?
- What is the individual's role with others in your network?
- How will you get the person to do what you want?
- What will you do with the person if you don't need him or her anymore?

## Function

This is about designing your network rather than letting it take shape.

Is your network like your Facebook page—the electronic version of a frat party? Or is your network creating strong bonds from real friends to reliable professional relationships that bring balance to your life and support your goals? You think that Facebook can do that? Very funny; get a different book.

I want to introduce you to new ways of understanding why networks exist and making key bonds even stronger to serve your purposes.

## Understanding the Landscape

Our training exercises for interrogators include assembling 100 people or more and instructing the interrogators to speak to them in whatever language the interrogators would use in a real situation. The interaction is similar to something they might encounter in the Middle East if 100 people were rounded up by going house to house. Most of them would be employees of the households.

People from all over the world are in Middle Eastern countries because they're looking for money. They have service jobs like many immigrants in the United States.

The younger guys in the exercises thought the scenario was crazy: "What a waste of time. That'll never happen." The senior guys who had been there told them, "It happens all the time."

A lesson integral to this exercise is that "the help" can often provide excellent intelligence, so you'd better find a way to communicate with them so that they do not feel inferior and do feel motivated to connect with you.

## You Are Not a Spy

Spies as we define them here are intelligence collectors who work the streets. The people they "work" are not their friends, family, and coworkers; they are sources. Even those sources can become such long-term acquaintances that the spy still needs to nurture the relationship.

Networking like a spy is not about using people. This is a process involving calculated decisions about where you focus your attention and how you use your time. It's about building and sustaining relationships that matter—not about gaining someone's trust only to later put that person in harm's way.

If you pair yourself with enough people whose success depends on your success, that's good networking. But as soon as you hang any one of those people out to dry, you damage your own reputation. You have to realize that the day you have to fire one of them, you taint your image in the process.

As an executive, the reason you do not want to bond with sycophants and idiots is because you heap scrutiny on yourself when you get tired of them and terminate them. Choose people who have the information, intelligence, and skills to contribute to your mission without embarrassing you or your company. But remember that, just like the poor uneducated Chinese maid in a rich Middle Eastern household, entry-level people add value to your company and therefore to your network. Networks are complex, with varying degrees of connection.

## *The Atomic Model*

A general note up front about the composition and character of your network: Even though recruiting peers may seem more appealing—it keeps you in your comfort zone—connecting with the superiors and subordinates and drawing them into your network is essential. And no matter who they are, remember that connections forged with trust and respect have the best chance of serving you well.

Networking like a spy is a chess game. First, you have to be able to differentiate your pieces from the opponent's. Second, it's a matter of knowing where your pieces are on the board and being aware at all times that you have to think several moves ahead to win. Third, you need to think in terms of order of importance. Some people in your network have a crucial role; others play a secondary or tertiary role. You need them all for different reasons. As you think about the model for an atom, you see a nucleus with electrons in orbits around the center. The complexity comes in that you share electrons with lots of other atoms. And you need to be keenly aware of which other orbits they are in and why.

You don't build 3-D networks with a Facebook or MySpace page, and you don't do it by limiting your view of the possibilities to a planar 360 degrees. Even LinkedIn, which provides professional benefits, has no relationship to networking like a spy. The popular Web-based networking sites are about taking advantage of other people's connections in a superficial way. You are not aiming for that kind of wide-open, public circle of "friends" here. You want meaningful elements to your network in four key categories. Just like the CIA case officer, you want to build a network of people who can collect and pass information, protect you, and warn you. Unlike the case officer, you cannot move treacherously through the world; your day job and your normal life won't allow that. Nonetheless, you need people who fill these four roles:

**Blockers** Some people are in your network for one reason: You need them to protect you. That protection can be in any form you can imagine. Some blockers are like a big dog on a chain. They are there, right out in the open, for the fear factor.

One of my long-time associates was consulting with a high-technology consortium and had a couple of good-humored—and genuinely respectful—encounters with a low-level guy in the office. He was a pleasant, smart, bumbling giant, and she just liked talking with him. It turned out that he was the son of the organization's board chairman. In a situation when she needed to change people's minds about how to do something, he became her bad dog on a chain. The relationship ended in a flash when he left the company a week later to take another job, but it had certainly served a purpose.

When I taught antiterrorism, we taught a very different version of the guard dog. Do not get a giant, fear-nothing attack dog. Get one that panics easily and let him wake you up to do the dirty work.

If all your dogs on chains are ferocious, the bad guys might get you. If you have some little nervous Chihuahuas that panic at footsteps, you'll get plenty of warning to bring the big dog out.

**Collectors** In the real world, agents are working sources of information. In your network, you will want sources, too. These are people who can sit in meeting you are not privy to and can go into places that you would not want to be, or help you get access to other sources of intelligence. Long-term intelligence collectors in business need to be the kind of people you can share with in confidence, and unless in the real spy business, the ones you trust as friends.

The short-term collectors take a different skill set to manage and often are simply gears in the machine, not even aware of the part they play.

You pick people as collectors for your network because of their

• Capability

and/or

• Proximity

Capability encompasses talent and skill in serving your intelligence needs. Proximity reflects connections and the judgments and emotions related to them. For example, you may have a grudge against your boss. You have access to him—you have proximity—and have value to me because your boss is my rival. The first is obvious. I'll give you an explicit example of the second.

When I was an Army interrogator with Arabic language skills assigned to a Special Forces unit in Operation Desert Storm, in the immediate aftermath of the war, there were tons of bad guys and literally hundreds of thousands of weapons still in the city. We lived in a Kuwaiti neighborhood near a police department and worked with the Kuwaiti army. In effect, that made me a counterintelligence guy, which means I was part of the effort to prevent hostile forces from getting the upper hand. Because of my intelligence training, I saw everyone as a potential source of information.

Kids would come around and hang out of with us every morning as we strolled around their neighborhood. It was fun for me because they spoke proper Arabic, which is what I knew, so we could have friendly banter. In fact, they helped improve my Arabic to a steady conversational level. One morning, I was standing outside of a police station handing out candy to the kids. They loved it; some of them had not had candy in a while. In fact, some of them hadn't had food in a while, so we'd share our MREs (Meals, Ready-to-Eat).

I had a rifle under my coat. One of the kids touched it, and I said, "Don't touch that; it's dangerous." My concern was that he would grab it and hurt himself, or me.

One of the other kids chimed in, "His daddy's got a lot of guns!"

I gave that kid extra candy. Part of our job was to disarm the city, so we visited the boy's daddy and took away his weapons.

The next day, another kid said, "His daddy's got guns, too" and pointed to another boy.

We were suspicious, but followed up and, sure enough: The kid may have been after more candy, but he was also right about the guns.

We understood that those people would want to hoard weapons because they had just been invaded, but our job as the leaders of a thirty-four–nation United Nations task force was to disarm everyone in sight who wasn't part of the coalition force.

**Support**   Clandestine officers categorize support folks as "assets." Anyone living a double life needs support if those around her are aware of her double identity. They try to maintain ties that are easy to sever or try to create cutouts. These people provide things like information about the best place to do a dead drop or where to plant a bug.

Your support people can be much more open and reliable. In fact, my friends are often my support people, lending me advice, trusted opinions, and a 360-degree look at the terrain around me. The unwitting support folks are drones you trick into doing things for you.

Another way to play people in your network negatively is called *false-flag recruitment* in the spy business.

Barbara was enamored with the company's flamboyant chief executive officer (CEO). She hoped that someday she would make a contribution that would catch his attention and give her direct access to him. It became a running joke in the break room that Barbara would run down the halls naked if she thought the CEO would appreciate it. John happened to overhear that. He needed someone with Barbara's marketing savvy on a special project. The only way he could get her on the team is if she asked for the temporary assignment, though.

John's mentor was a member of the board who wanted to take down the CEO and the special project was a political move to show the CEO's Achilles' heel. But when John approached Barbara about helping, he made a convincing case for how desperately the CEO needed the project to succeed. If it didn't, his strategic vision would be under scrutiny. In good faith, she plunged into the project with all her creative energy and skills.

Once entrenched in the project, Barbara discovered the hidden agenda, but backing out would probably mean being fired. She was stuck. This is the nature of false-flag recruitment: Someone pretends to represent the cause you espouse, but in actuality, is recruiting you for the other side. This kind of underhanded dealing is highly dangerous for all involved and should be treated as such.

**Terminators** You might think of these people as a kind of support or blocker, but they actually have a different and unique purpose. Terminators help you end other relationships, usually in a straightforward and easy manner. They may be temporary members of your network recruited specifically to eliminate someone else from your network. Or they may be people you know will leak information that leads to someone being pushed from the group. There are multiple variations.

I have good friends who hate each other's guts. To avoid conflict, I never invite them to the same party. That kind of relationship management is common. Consider that you can deliberately invite someone to your party who is disliked by someone else who's coming. You can terminate the relationship with that latter person—if not both—just by putting them at the same hors d'oeuvre table together. You can do that if you've determined that those relationships will be short term. You build in a trip wire so you can get rid of both of them.

The Kuwaiti kids trading guns for caramels were just such targets because of proximity.

Think about the part each of these people plays. Are they trusted advisors, mentors, confidants, or casual acquaintances you have seen so many times that you feel you have a bond? Put all of the people in your world into a 3-D atomic model. Who is orbiting close to you, and who shouldn't even be there?

As long as your mission is clear so you know the type of people you need to have in place in your network, your recruitment efforts for long-term connections are ongoing. You may not know the specific people you want, but you know the kind of people and are set up to bring them in.

When you work in intelligence, there is a ton of produced material that is kept on file; someday it may be useful. At the beginning of the chapter, I referenced Polish Colonel Ryszard Kuklinski. When he volunteered to aid the United States in 1971, the CIA already had a dusty file on him. In 1967, when he had been sent on a peacekeeping mission to Vietnam, he had a favorable encounter with a U.S. intelligence officer who documented the exchange and sent his notes home to Langley. When Kuklinski later reached out, the CIA had background on him.

The smart spy has confidential resources collected and organized like the Kuklinski file, as well as a handle on relevant resources that are openly available. When a potential "Mr. Right" comes through the door, all she has to do is access them to get a running start on establishing contact.

What exactly do you know about your "friend" Joe at Starbucks—all fired up on the caffeine and overhearing everyone's cell phone conversations? Always there to greet you with a high-energy, nervous smile?

## Tools of Networking
### *Elicitation Techniques*

*Studies in Intelligence,* the "Journal of the American Intelligence Professional," has plenty of articles on how to recruit. At one time, the articles in the journal had classifications that allowed only active clandestine officers access to them. One is George G. Bull's article on elicitation techniques that appeared in the fall 1970 issue.

Bull was serving in West Germany when he documented the process of elicitation in the recruitment process for his fellow officers in the clandestine service. He zeroed in on the "practical problems" they face in collecting human intelligence, or HUMINT. The five main problems he addressed were:

1. Finding a reason to talk to the source
2. Locating the source
3. Positively identifying the person as the one you want
4. Maintaining cover during the encounter
5. Keeping the source focused on the subject you want to discuss

Using his stories from the field, he then talked about how to apply elicitation techniques successfully.

**Targeting**   After identifying who belongs in your network, consider the tools to solve practical problems in your recruiting action. Some of these are the tools Bull discussed, and some come from me.

Let's solve the five problems:

**1. Finding a reason to talk to the source**  In other words, why would he want to talk to *me*? The answer: because I want him to talk to me. Here are three tools I use to engender that opportunity for connection.

*Reptilian Creatures of Opportunity Lie in Wait*  When an enemy combatant is taken into custody, a support solider is responsible for that prisoner's basic needs. This means that at the time of induction into a prison camp, a soldier will approach the prisoner with a checklist to find out the prisoner's shoe size, shirt size, and so on. Often the enemy prisoner doesn't speak English, and the only interpreters in the compound are interrogators. These interrogators support the induction team by interpreting.

When we dealt with enemy combatants in the first Gulf War, as members of military intelligence, we would have been idiots to interpret the questions literally because our core job is to collect intelligence, not to come up with the Arabic phrase for "What's your shoe size?" So by saying something such as, "This guy is going to take care of your clothes and food, so he needs to know a few things to help you," we could set the stage for intelligence collection. We'd start with something such as, "First of all, what's your unit?"

The prisoner doesn't see the support soldier as a threat and the interrogator is helping that soldier, so he doesn't see the interrogator as a threat either. In the course of getting the facts the support soldier needs, the interrogator sucks information out of the prisoner. As someone aimed at collecting intelligence, I see the prisoner as fitting into my short-term network because I will likely get some piece of the puzzle from him that relates to the mission. I might never see this person again—or I might be the person who interrogates him for months. I must understand how the future interaction will play out as a result of this first interchange and where he will fit into my network for the long haul.

The real key is to keep the support soldier from ever knowing it happened so that he does not inadvertently telegraph his awareness to the next guy. Often these support people would think us bottom-feeders if they knew what we were doing, and they would unintentionally bleed that information to the prisoner via action or body language.

The equivalent in your business is finding a reason the person *needs* to talk to you and then transitioning to techniques to create a bond. This is simply applying some forethought to getting an audience.

Sometimes, you need to be creative in determining who might have that kind of information; they do not just "appear" like that enemy combatant.

**Be a Vampire: Create Your Own Opportunity**  When things were collapsing in Bosnia in 1996, I helped our forces relocate civilians in the United States. One of the skills I contributed was experience in relating to and processing people with whom I have no language in common. The soldiers appreciated how that ability made their lives easier when the buses of Bosnians arrived at Fort Dix, but they still didn't want to trust me because I was an intelligence guy and soldiers typically distrusted those of us working in intelligence jobs. The assumption is that their aims would become secondary to our desire to walk into their operation for the sole purpose of extracting information. Because of that, they referred to us as vampires. As soon as they found out I was an intelligence guy who served with Special Forces units, however, they trusted that I would stay true to their mission.

We had a very limited number of linguists for the native languages of people from Bosnia but an abundance of interpreters for other languages on site. I proposed putting up large poster boards in the different languages saying, "If you speak Spanish, take a blue card," "If you speak French, take a green card," and so on, so that interpreters who happened to speak these languages could communicate with the displaced persons' using their secondary language. Not only did this allow the refugees to find help, but it also allowed us to understand who we had on site, to network because they had a language in common with us, and to ask questions such as, "By the way, as a refugee from Bosnia, how is it that you happen to speak Mandarin?"

The other soldiers weren't the only ones who appreciated this scheme. The other government officials on the team might have liked my idea if they could have seen past my role. When I was introduced to the government official as an interrogator, I was sent back to my office, tagged a vampire.

In a situation analogous to this, you create your own opportunities by looking for points of difference that make the person stand out from the others, as well as what differences from what is expected for the group. You create an artificial bond when you find something that you have in common with that person that even his own people find odd. These differences can be highly contrived and yet seem very natural.

**2. Locating the Source**   When a spy wants someone specific in her network, she will put assets around him in a spherical fashion. She will put in place the people she needs above, below, and all around him to get a complete picture of the individual. In some cases, she may even pay thugs she doesn't want a relationship with if those people have access to a view of her target that completes her understanding of him. Think of these thugs as pawns on the 3-D chessboard. She then brings the source into the network.

If you get enough information about the things surrounding a person, you can build a relatively good picture of the person you are looking at without having direct knowledge of him. The effect is similar to the 3-D models created from Pin Art devices, which are made up of lots of pins; if someone were to press on it with his hand and deliver the model to you, you would have a good likeness of his hand without ever seeing it. For example, you may find that when you are simply talking to people who know your target, they start to wince or knit their brows when they say his name. That's as good as a billboard announcing he is going to be a pain in the ass to deal with. Conversely, if people you get along with have pleasant things to say about him, then he probably won't be a pain in the ass to deal with. In either case, you are looking to get a well-rounded, four-color picture of whether or not he is the guy you need.

**3. Positively Identifying the Person as the One You Want**   Use casual conversation to determine the person's expertise and value to you. This isn't complicated; it's really just baiting and listening. The following technique may help, even if you're a little shy.

*Five Questions to Common Ground*   Consider this technique a warm-up for using elicitation skills. This is a way to center a conversation, and I teach it to nearly all my classes. I find that it's particularly useful to people who don't naturally connect with others. My five-questions technique tends to ease people together more naturally than something like the "three-foot rule."

When I first began consulting with a particular company, I encountered the three-foot rule. Over the years, I've heard many variations on what this implies. To some companies, it means that anyone within three feet of you will hear about your company and its products and services. In a strip club, it means you don't get closer than three feet to a dancer or some Hell's Angel bouncer will throw you out the door. In this company, it meant that an employee should never be standing three feet from someone and not know something about him. The point was to get their people to network, but the implementation challenged some people beyond their abilities.

Interrogators use a version of the five-questions technique, and so do good journalists, interviewers, and anyone else who has a need to build connections efficiently. The objective: Take any topic and in just five questions move it to something you know about. If you meet a person who is smarter than you on a particular topic and you want to be perceived as intelligent or valuable, you need to take the topic at hand and recenter the conversation on something you are knowledgeable about.

Here is one way it played out in an exercise with an employee at Trane.

My work with Trane began with operations teams, which are typically composed of people who are gray matter people. They demonstrate value primarily by knowing how to install, maintain, and fix things. One of the people in my class was undoubtedly one of the brightest people in the company. Role-playing with her illustrated how hard it was for her to follow the company's three-foot rule. Here's how it went:

"Hello, I'm Greg."

"Hi, I'm Jane. What do you do for a living?" (Question 1)

"I'm a biochemist."

For her, the conversation stopped there. Jane had been in the air-conditioning business since she was 19 years old. She rose through the ranks in operations and could go even further if she simply mastered this skill of networking. The breakthrough that helped her do it took surprisingly little time.

I told her the next question could be, "What do you do as a biochemist?" (Question 2)

"I work in a pharmaceutical company and so research."

"That sounds interesting. I have always been fascinated by the clean rooms you folks work in. What goes into making a space a clean room?" (Question 3)

"It's a combination of a lot of factors, but it starts with climate control—"

"Oh, of course. You have to have the right ambient temperature and filters for dust, don't you?" (Question 4)

"Absolutely!"

"I'm an equipment specialist for Trane Corporation and we configure some of those very units you need. Tell me about how you see your needs evolving in this area?" (Question 5)

Suddenly, the conversation is no longer about his being a biochemist. It's about air-conditioning, and she's on her home turf. She has a chance to add value to his knowledge, and the two of them have a common framework for talking about something that's important to both of them.

That maneuver gives her the confidence she needs to move on to other topics. After that initial exchange, which contains some substance, they can move on comfortably to family, golf, or whatever else comes up. If she had started with a question about family, though, it could have seemed intrusive, as in, "Hi, I'm Jane. Do you have kids?"

Sometimes, it's easy to fast-track the process if you just listen for cues. When Maryann was at the International Spy Museum chatting about body language, a woman came up and mentioned that her body language training came from learning to sing opera. Maryann didn't even have to show off any expertise in body language to forge a connection with her. She simply said, "You must know how to relax on cue to be an opera singer. Your vocal mechanisms need to stay open no matter how much pressure you're under. Could you please tell everyone how you do that?" The singer then taught everyone listening how she relaxes despite her stage fright.

Usually it's two or three questions to find common ground with someone, but anyone can learn to do it in no more than five. I could find something in common with Charles Manson by using this technique. It takes away judgmental behavior even if you are still judging the person. People will feel as though you are moving closer to them, and not judging them, no matter what they've done.

Police investigators do it, intelligence gatherers do it, interrogators do it, and you will find it useful as you go about deliberately building your network.

With the common ground established and the new member of your network in place, you are in a position to starting using your asset. Sometimes, there is a reason to use a person as a temporary asset; for example, you might want to extract information from the source without the person knowing about it.

**4. Maintaining Cover During the Encounter** One of your "double agents," that is, someone who is on your side but whom others perceive might be on theirs, might have an orbit that coincides with that of your nemesis in the finance department. Perhaps this person is not really a friend and not even on the periphery of your network; she's more of a water-cooler acquaintance and you are not sure you can trust her. You might want to collect information without her knowledge for that reason.

- Make idle chatter with her until you get a solid baseline.
- When you see the conversation is running smoothly, then move to the family of information you want, such as trends, and then to the specific information you want.
- When you get what you want, don't hop off the topic; chat a bit longer and go back out to the general information again until one or both of you decides it's time to finish.

Steer the conversation using one or more of these tools:

- Arranging a quid pro quo, that is, giving something like information or money in exchange for something you value—It's a trade, but it may not be a one-to-one trade. You may dress up your information in an attractive package to make it appear special and, in offering that, get insider information you can really use.

- Showing deference—A person who feels superior to you is often inclined to leak a little information to reinforce his value. You make him feel he clearly knows more than you do; maybe you convince him you don't even understand what he's talking about so he explains it more thoroughly.
- Mildly criticizing something, especially from a point of ignorance—This will quickly get someone to set you straight. You appeal to emotion, not thinking.
- Playing the expert—Taking the information you have, you can illustrate a rather clear understanding of the issue and leave out the fact you don't know detail X. Through conversation, the source assumes you know everything and when you are finished, you do.

*Countering Elicitation*    What happens when you unwittingly become the source? You can recognize the techniques.

I could give you my own version of what you need to look out for and how to handle the situation, but instead I'm going to put my tax dollars to work (and maybe yours as well) and get the answer from the Department of Homeland Security. This is available freely online:

**What to Do**

If you ever feel that you are being drawn into a conversation that makes you uncomfortable, keep these points in mind:

- You are not obliged to tell people any information they are not authorized to hear; that includes personal information about you or your colleagues.
- You can simply ignore any question you think is improper and change the topic.
- You can deflect the question with one of your own.
- You can give a nondescript answer.
- You can simply say that you do not know.
- If all else fails, you can state that you would have to clear such discussions with your Security Office.

Or in your case just get up and walk out or spill your drink— anything to change the subject.

**5. Keeping the Source Focused on the Subject You Want to Discuss** When you are trying to collect information without broadcasting what you want, you need to corral the conversation. The elicitation tools combined with a couple of others will help you keep the source you don't quite trust on target without the person knowing you're probing. You want the source to give you the information without knowing what you're really focused on.

- Engage in active listening—You can bring up a topic and show your genuine interest in what the person says by "speaking" with your body. While you remain almost silent, your body participates in the conversation with nods and smiles.
- Get them talking—Salespeople are often taught that people love the sound of their name more than anything. Not so. They love the sound of their own voice. Or put them on topic they love and release the brakes.

When a friend of mine who was on staff at a children's museum needed $25,000 for an after-school program for latchkey kids, she made an appointment with the senior executive of a publishing company. She thought the donation would give the company good publicity, but more than that, she had targeted the executive, a man known for his sensitivity to kids in need. She began the meeting by asking him to tell her about another program for children he supported. For the next hour, she hardly said a word—but she did get the $25,000.

At this point, thanks to a combination of Mr. Bull's insights and mine, you have your target in your network or have exploited a double-agent source. What now?

# Motivating Behavior

Look for a person's innate motivation. The Kuwaiti kid who jumped at the chance to turn in his friend's parents was a clear HELP ME revolutionary as far as his friends were concerned, but he set a precedent and his friends joined in. Take the Kuwaiti kid's story and add a grudge to the same scenario. In that case, you would have people who will go out of their way to expose someone or leak information. They might want a reward—whatever their "candy" is—but they might divulge what they know just because "hate of" something or someone is driving them to help you punish them. Often, going into a foreign country with oppressed people, you have individuals at all levels of power willing to collaborate because of ideology. They beg you to recruit them. They go out of their way to find a market for the information they have.

You have to be very careful about information like that. In Chapter 6, on researching like an analyst, you will see guidelines on vetting sources to avoid being duped.

When you collect information from someone who is disgruntled, he's waiting for an action in response. Some people will wait a long time for revenge. Others want their reward instantly, and if they don't get it, they will leak their information to someone else—or just let it be known that you are armed with acid. It's dangerous to deal with people carrying a grudge. Move them out of your network as soon as they have fulfilled their purpose.

Start with trust. As long as you have a bond of trust with people in your network—for as long as they are there, whether that's 20 minutes or 20 years—you have a high degree of confidence that those people are playing on your side. Because trust is so fundamental to your network development, you might want someone in your network just because you like her, not because she can serve as intelligence collector or someone who can block an attack. The professional trade you make is that you want to do things for her to make her life better, and that's what she will do for you. Whatever that may be. Not only is there nothing wrong with that, there is everything right with networking with someone for whom you have respect.

To spend one sentence on the obvious: You need your first-tier people to get what you want efficiently. People in the orbit around them make your job easier. But your network might also include people you would not normally think of as having a bearing on your professional success: those from outside your organization. These are folks like your Rotary buddies and sorority sisters, who all have some desirable influence on your life.

You can put them in play. You should put them in play as long as your goal is consistent with their values and interests.

## Moving Someone to Action

Two real factors motivate most human beings: The first is progress along Maslow's Hierarchy of Needs, and the second is love, hate, or greed as the primary emotion in dealing with issues.

### The Foundation: Belonging and Differentiating  In 1943, psychologist Abraham Maslow posited that we move from physiological needs, up to safety needs, up another step to the need to belong, up another level to esteem, and finally to self-actualization at the top. (Refer to Figure 1.2 in Chapter 1.) One level of needs must be fulfilled before the next can be attained. Most people spend their lives trying to belong and differentiate; that is, we hang around levels three and four. Like big fish outgrowing their pond, they get into new groups and then become a bigger fish in the new pond.

If you can help move someone along in that transition, then you have an edge in drawing that person into your circle and creating a mutually beneficial relationship.

### The Fulfillment Strategy  The Fulfillment Strategy is straightforward:

- Determine what value the person has. In some cases, value is in plain sight; in others, it is well hidden. Use the elicitation tools to draw it out.
- Discover the person's levers, that is, what will motivate the individual to demonstrate his value.
- Reward the person accordingly so that he feels fulfilled.

People at the top of their heap have little incentive to commit to your network unless you enable them to get to the next level of fulfillment. A number of Soviet defectors had power and rank when they chose to aid the United States. For example, Soviet diplomat Arkady Shevchenko, the highest-ranking defector throughout the Cold War, took an enormous risk in crossing over, and he lost his wife in the process. His ideology drove him to take that step, so he no doubt felt elevated through the defection; of course, he also had no problems taking advantage of the physical comforts and bonuses that his elite status gave him with the CIA and Federal Bureau of Investigation (FBI). His handlers knew exactly how to get him to the next level of fulfillment.

Sometimes you find a person who holds all the keys and works in relative obscurity, akin to the Keymaker in *The Matrix Reloaded*. The Keymaker is the sentient rogue program that carves shortcut keys used by programs in the Matrix and whom Neo seeks out. Neo's objective is to get the key to the back door of the Architect of the matrix and ultimately save the human world of Zion.

In some cases the key maker is moved to obscurity by the way the organization operates. In others, he is in plain sight and no one can see him because he is known for something else. When this happens, the key maker gets dispatched to a small room and his personal fulfillment is hindered. You can choose to simply visit his room, take the key he has that you need, and leave him working. Or you can construct a path to success for both of you. Instead of simply taking the key he offers you, you take him with you and teach people to think of him in a new way. You introduce a wider audience to the array of talents he has. That effectively moves him up a level on the hierarchy to a state of differentiation. Your action can create a long-term bond that enables you to take advantage of his talents again at a later date. Fulfilling his needs at the same time you fulfill your own might start off as simply a work relationship, but you might also find out that if you work with people in this kind of respectful mutually beneficial way, you create more than simply a work relationship.

You can think of this as manipulation—the positive kind.

**The Factors of Fulfillment** Think back to the action matrix and where people are on it. Their action styles are tied up in three factors that create equilibrium to maintain stability: passion, trust, and hope.

• Passion

A person can live her life in relative obscurity, happy to trudge along, if she is not passionate about anything. She can wander the planet and never take a single action. She's just happy to breathe the air.

The minute you add passion for a given subject, that changes. You have seen it, and probably felt it, as people discover a new hobby or lover, or they get the job of their dreams. Passion takes that lifeless canvas and creates a new billboard for whatever engenders the passion.

That is the positive kind of passion. When someone feels wronged, either for herself or others, the dark side of passion emerges. Fueled by anger and intensity to right the wrong, this passion pushes the person deeper into the action style she is in, or the one you intend to move her to.

- Trust

I often say fear is the most mind-numbing of narcotics. In the immediate wake of the 9/11 attacks, most Americans began to trust the government in ways we have not in decades. The fear of uncertainty about what was coming next and how we would deal with it created a need to trust our government and write blank checks for what needed to be done. That kind of faith in the system created an opportunity for the legislators (in the Chapter 1 *and* the government sense) to build toward a vision of whatever brand of better they envisioned. Then one afternoon, that fear-inspired trust wore off. If you are an American and thinking, "That wasn't me!" then you're one of a handful. More likely, you have obliterated that feeling. When the scares stopped, the trust came crashing down for many of us as we started hearing about wiretapping and other domestic spying activities. Most people trust the system when it is beneficial for them to trust the system on a micro level (for example, office) or macro level (for example, government or church).

Fear is a great lever to force a need for trust, whether the fear is from a tangible enemy like terrorism or one more insidious, such as homelessness, poverty, and hunger. When that trust is violated or we open our eyes and see it is simply not deserved, we lose faith in the thing we trusted. Loss of faith in a system moves people from positive to negative energy, and passion determines how far.

• Hope

"Disappointment is a sort of bankruptcy—the bankruptcy
of a soul that expends too much in hope and expectation."
—Eric Hoffer

Hope can be an impatient or a patient thing. It runs from a
child who hopes the surprise his mom has promised is in the bag
she is holding to the kind of hope it takes to become a CEO. No
person in life goes about his daily life like one of the kids in the
Monster.com ad saying, "I want to claw my way up to middle
management." We all move into the workforce with expectations
or hopes. We align our arrows to the best of our abilities and tackle
obstacles and jump hurdles, all of the while keeping hope in mind.

When we wake up one morning to find that all of that hope in
the back of or heads was overinvested, we become disillusioned.
The impact is devastating. In political terms, it creates revolution;
in business terms, high attrition. Hope is a tool to be managed. It
can set real expectations with timelines that are practical and create
dedicated long-term relationships, or it can engender fervor to
action. On the simplest level, it's the child madly cleaning his
room to get that trip to McDonald's. On the complex side, it's a
mother whose children are out of the house and who goes back to
school with the hope of not only earning more money but also
obtaining fulfillment to move up Maslow's Hierarchy of Needs.
Masterful manipulation of hope can move the masses to actions.
Fumbling with someone's hope creates chaos at best and hostage
situations—real or figurative—at worst. Loss of hope drives a
person from enduring to impatient and vice versa. The level of
passion determines how far.

## Tools of Influence

Realizing where a person fits in Maslow's Hierarchy of Needs is the
first key (see Figure 3.1). Is your target struggling to get to acceptance by a peer group? Or is he busy differentiating himself from
the group? Remember, this can be going on in multiple groups or

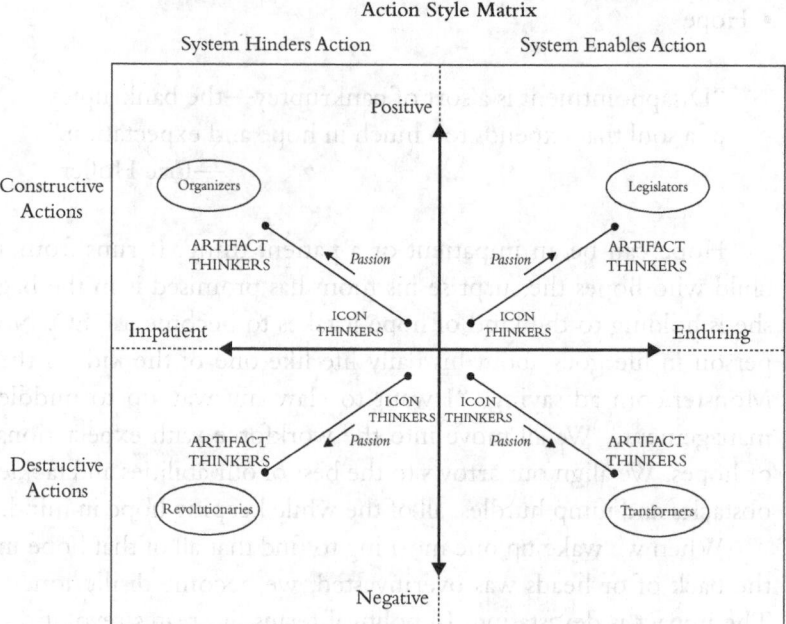

**FIGURE 3.1** You can change action styles of a person by managing trust, hope, and passion.

networks simultaneously, so you need to be a keen observer of who he is and where he fits today. By understanding that, you can ascertain how to drive his action style. By determining his rewards and expectations, you can use a few specific tools to affect each of the three axes: hope, trust, and passion.

> "It is the around-the-corner brand of hope that prompts people to action, while the distant hope acts as an opiate."
> —Eric Hoffer

Managing the axis of endurance is about setting expectations that are either realistic and deliverable within a given timeline *or* unrealistic and too difficult to understand—and then pushing the person to lose hope.

Some people see the big picture clearly; they have a good idea how to climb to the next level of the hierarchy. That makes them enduring. They walk around never losing hope. I had a conversation a few years ago with the then–vice president of service for

Trane about just such hope. He had been a professional baseball player for a short time as a young man. When that ended, he wanted a job in the Trane HVAC business. He interviewed for a position as a service technician, even though that was not the job he wanted. When the manger of that district office asked him, "What is it then that you *do* want to do?" He answered, "I want your job." And that is what he does today. That kind of vision or hope takes strategy, planning, and a good network to accomplish. It is not in itself the kind of immediate gratification that Hoffer is talking about, but along the way, this man had numerous successes toward that ultimate goal. Each kept his hope burning. Rest assured that others around him drew on his hope to accomplish short- and long-term goals for themselves.

Others can have the idea of what they want for the long term and yet not understand that it is composed of steps that may be inherently frustrating. Along the way, even brilliant people can mire in mediocrity as a result. With your eye on someone like that as a target, your choice is whether to disillusion her—you take away her hope and drive her to action—or to give her finite tasks that can put her on track and maintain hope. The latter keeps her in the enduring disposition category. Even the most enduring people will jump to immediacy, of course, when they see the loss of hope. It is the great catalyst.

Managing the axis of positive and negative energy is about managing trust.

I once had a commander who wanted to pull his team together. His cadre consisted of Special Forces, interrogators, and support people, almost all of whom were the same rank. In light of their persistent infighting, he asked my opinion about drawing the group together. I told him we needed an outside enemy to take us off the differentiating actions we were feverishly undertaking. He did exactly that. He became the "enemy." Just like Americans after 9/11, we pulled together to overcome that enemy. The Army gives authoritarian rule, so he was in less danger than you would be with the same ploy in your company. Through creating that need to trust others around us, he forced us to work together.

You can improve trust through tools other than fear as well. By making promises that are succinct and tied to the person's Maslow desires, and quickly fulfilling those promises, you engender trust.

Sometimes information is all that is needed. Think about the conspiracy theorist who believes that the U.S. government is keeping aliens hidden away in some work camp in Nevada. Simple logic should tell him that having aliens living next door to The Strip would differentiate us as a culture a lot more than landing on the moon. But because there is void of information, they can fill in the blanks and create mistrust and questions even in some sane people. When we throw open intelligence documents with open investigations into these reports of aliens, we bring those sane people back into the model of trust.

Conversely, quick to promise and slow to fulfill triggers a lack of trust and belief that the current system or relationship is not reliable, and the belief it needs to be replaced or worked around. When the report released has huge sections redacted, the conspiracy theorists start to gain ground again. Only when someone credible explains that the blacked out bits are about how the government collects intelligence, and not what the intelligence is, do we see movement toward reinserting some trust in the relationship.

Now turn to the passion axis.

As both interrogators and spies know well, three emotions drive most of our behaviors and arouse the strongest passion: "love of," "hate of," and greed. A person may be driven by love of country, family, God, money, applause, pandas, vodka, and so on. A person may be driven by hate of your country, your family, your God, your money, your vodka, and so on.

The concept of greed may seem foreign, but give some thought to combining this with the endurance factor and what you know about climbing Maslow's Hierarchy of Needs. If the pursuit of money would interrupt the drive upward on the hierarchy, then it will not spark passion. But if money is tied to his Maslow aims, then pursuit of it will drive passion. You can drive him to the edge of the matrix.

Use the disposition matrix included to get clearer on how to move people around (see Figure 3.2). The closer a person is to the center of the $x/y$-axis, the harder you have to work to influence behavior. As he gets farther away, your job gets easier because ideology comes into play more; this is how fanatics are bred.

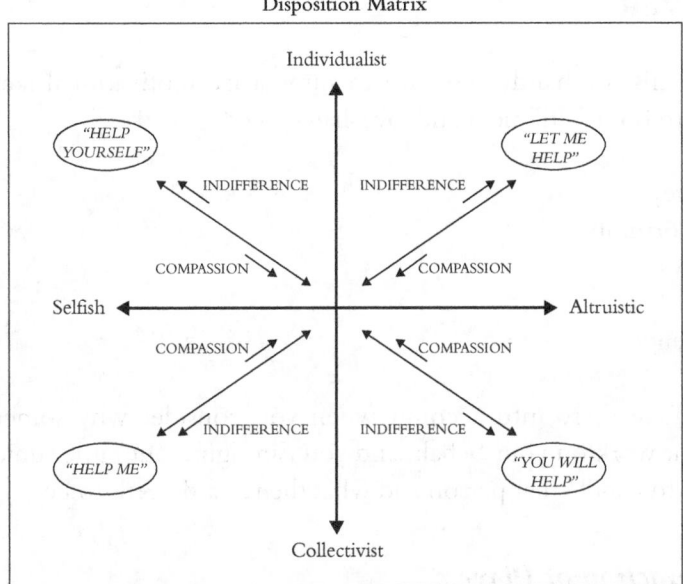

**FIGURE 3.2** The closer a person is to the inside, the harder it is to influence his behavior.

By learning these feelings, you can drive a person to a point of passion or drive her to do something she would not normally do, like the young woman driven to meet the CEO who unwittingly helps sabotage him instead. She is a person with such tunnel vision that, when she sees opportunity to get his attention, will miss the nature of the true situation that's hidden in plain sight.

Fear removes the thinking brain, and you do not need to be in full-blown fight or flight to lose the use of your frontal lobe.

Look for the pieces that indicate how a person is wired in disposition, and then look for deviations in the baseline as you talk until you find a hot button. You can choose to bond with her by helping her overcome her enemy in the process, relieving her stress, and bringing her fight or flight down. Alternatively, you can string her along with elusive promises of what you have to offer. Either way, you can use her type and other details you have discovered, watch her body language for signs of acceptance or rejection, and reward her or punish her along the way.

**MOVER**

This is a handy acronym to summarize motivational factors tied to both fulfillment and love-hate-greed.

**M**oney
**O**pportunity
**V**alues
**E**go
**R**evenge

Take these into account when you consider why someone might work on your behalf, and you can figure out rather quickly how to handle that person and what the reward needs to be.

## Interaction of Players

What is the job of everyone in your network—support, intelligence, blocker, or terminator?

If your long-term objective is to be the director of operations for an entire business unit at your multibillion-dollar company—and that's really what you care about accomplishing—then you will recruit people into your network who will provide either information or influence to get there. In complementary ways, those people will give you a 3-D picture of whom and what you need to succeed. You will also need people to look out for your interests by running interference or taking a direct hit to prevent you from losing face.

The dynamics change dramatically depending on the situation.

Maryann had a boss who exploited the fact that people liked her by making her the messenger for bad news. The premise was, if she shows up at your door, how bad could the bad news be? She was essentially a human minimizer: an executioner who made you feel taken care of. She could move things along in the company in a way that the boss couldn't because his involvement would have automatically triggered fear and resentment.

I've played a similar role. While my boss had a reputation of being forceful and mean, even though I could be just as forceful and mean, my role was to go into an office with bad news and disarm the person. I was junior to the boss, so they did not perceive me as a threat—regardless of the sharp knife I carried.

And don't make the assumption that people in your network will always get along; in fact, sometimes your objective is that they do not.

Only when you understand the complexity of your networks and of the talents of the people therein can you begin to think of how they fit or if they fit, and when they don't, when to terminate them.

CHAPTER 4

# Interview Like an
# Interrogator

**Tools**
- Screening
- Planning and preparation
- Establishment of control
- Rapport building
- Approaches
- Questioning techniques
- Behavioral interviewing
- Termination

Interrogations are contrived meetings with one person trying to get key information in a timely fashion and the other either cooperating or trying to hide it. The key difference in an interrogation is that most of the time, the "interviewee" doesn't want the relationship to continue.

I will share information that is based on the huge number of interrogations I've conducted and that captures effective practices from having been an interviewer and interviewee in some of the best and worst interviews ever.

## Value to Business

Get the right person to replace the revolutionary you terminated after reading Chapter 1 because of her fervor to overthrow your "government."

This chapter primarily addresses how to conduct an interview so that you understand how the job candidate deals with stress and what intent lies behind the conversation. It's applying the tools to assess disposition and action style to determine how someone fits into your organization.

Also, interrogation is a type of meeting, so it needs to have a structure that allows you to drive toward a meaningful conclusion. I've laid out that structure, which is one that I have used very effectively in business meetings for years.

## Tools of Interviewing

### Screening

Sort through the masses efficiently to find the person you want.

We usually have at least dozens, if not hundreds or thousands, of prisoners per interrogator. Not all of those sources have valuable information. Even if they do, we can't talk to all of them.

In the interrogation world, we have intelligence collection requirements written by analysts that tell us what they want to know. These requirements are not all-inclusive laundry lists of intelligence gaps; rather, they are often categories of information we need. They are broken into priority intelligence requirements (PIRs) and information requirements (IRs).

The PIRs are key things you truly need. Whether it's intelligence information that gives insights into the local situation or theater-level information, these are usually the facts and perspectives that will bite you in the ass if you don't know them.

In an interview, prioritize what you're after. Do you really want to hear about a time that the candidate was brilliant, or is it more important to know how honest she is or how she reacts to stress?

Intelligence screening is a process of assigning a code based on two factors:

1. How likely it is the person will cooperate
   1 = No psychology needed; just ask
   2 = Psychological ploys needed
   3 = Forget it
   In the intelligence world, we call this cooperability.
2. What the person will probably know based on experience and exposure
   We assign a letter code that reflects the level of the person's knowledge.
   A = Can provide PIRs
   B = Can provide IRs
   C = Has no intelligence value
   In the intelligence world, we call this letter knowledgeability.

Interrogators all want the "1A," a guy who can get the job done and is easy to work with. Sound familiar?

These are the two categories the intelligence world uses. You might take this same approach to screening all of the applicants you get. And you can use it more than once in the process. For instance, to decide whether experience in the industry and time in the same job matters most, you can provide a set of filters for screening résumés. And then, after you get to the interview process, apply a new set of filters such as "personality match" as the number and "knowledge" as the letter. The deciding factor often is the sheer volume of applicants to screen.

For now, let's take the experience in the industry and time in position format. Use the letter grade for time in industry:

A = More than five years
B = One to five years
C = No industry experience

Use the number grade for time in the same job:

1 = More than five years in similar position
2 = One to five years in similar position
3 = No experience in similar position

Good interrogation units understand the value of intuition and insight in screening. You want human beings with excellent human–being skills to evaluate sources. Weaker interrogation units assign new people to screen because they view it as a job dependent on a rudimentary checklist. This is the same as your allowing your human resources (HR) team to screen résumés without a subject matter expert (SME) involved in the process.

Armed with screening reports, we prioritize people for "interview." We know we can't interview everybody, so we streamline the process using the tool shown in Figure 4.1. You can easily adapt this to your own uses by changing the two key factors. Instead of "pertinent knowledge" and "expected cooperation," for example, the factors could become "desirable action style" and "experience," or you might create other tags.

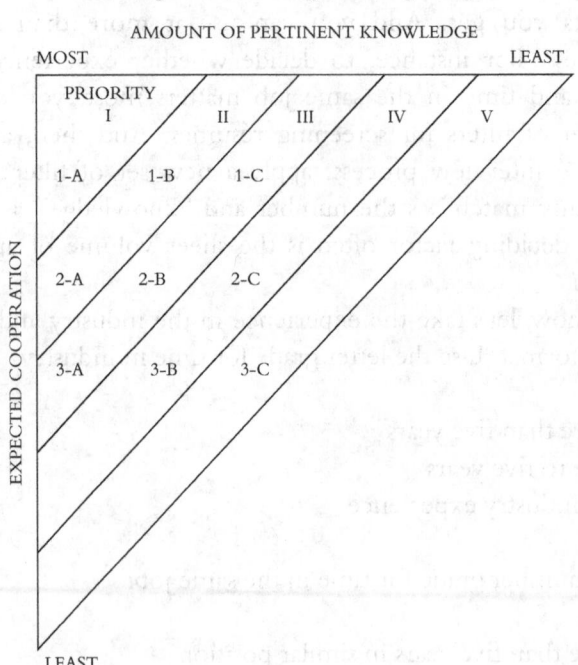

Interrogation Priorities by Screening Categories

FIGURE 4.1   Where are you on the continuum?

## *Planning and Preparation*

As interrogators, once we have narrowed the field to our "candidate for interview," we start planning and preparation by looking extensively at where the prisoner was captured and what was going on at the time, as well as who else being held was captured in an area close to him. We read reports on those other people, too. We examine all of the prisoner's belongings to build a solid 3-D image of who we are talking to before we start the interrogation. In business, you would ask others in your office who might have worked with the candidate in the past and do a web search of the person's name and see what pops up.

We also go to the analysts and ask for any information they have. They search databases and look for connections to organizations and activities so that we can get a grasp of his network. The corollary for you is using HR to keep you legal while you research all available connections to create a picture of the candidate long before you go into the interview room. Does she blog? Has she written any white papers? The key point here is to look at what you can find within legal parameters.

As part of planning and preparation, we decide on questioning strategy and who we will have in the room. If we need another interrogator or a guard, or even another prisoner, we need to start coordination at the outset. In your situation, the analogous issue is deciding who else should be involved and how: team interview? round-robin? Or will you use one of the scripted tools from HR or another free-interview tool?

We then plan our approach strategy. This involves thinking about whether we need a ploy to get the person to talk. Your ploy is she wants a job. You still might need some of these tools as you conduct the interview, though; in fact, they're key to determining personality and fit. Use what's relevant and natural given the circumstances. They have particular value in redirecting a conversation that's taken on too much heat.

## Main Interrogation Approaches as Applied to Business

Official manuals used by interrogators list a few other approaches, but these are the main ones that you will find useful:

1. Direct—A straightforward question: "How many units did you sell?"
2. Incentive—Offering a person something he really wants, like a raise or promotion.
3. Emotional—Using a desire to protect and defend, or to exact revenge, as leverage: "If you side with me in the meeting, I'll make sure your assistant doesn't get laid off."
4. Fear-up—Raising the stress level to get the desired result: "Would you rather help me with this project, or have me tell your boss that you play video games at the office?"
5. Fear-down—Reducing the stress level to get the desired result: "I know you're behind on that; let me help you make the deadline."
6. Pride-and-ego (up or down)—Complimenting or criticizing to manipulate the person's ego: "I can't believe someone as smart as you has to report to that moron," or "How did you get this job? I thought you had to at least be a college graduate."
7. Futility—Preying on doubts that anything can be done: "You might as well give me that account right now because you know you've done nothing but screw it up so far."
8. "We know all"—Using knowledge you have to make it appear you know so much there is no reason to hide anything from you.
9. Repetition—Asking essentially the same question over and over. I covered the concept in the section on questioning styles in Chapter 2. A repeat question is not redundant; it is a rephrasing of the question that allows you to drill down when you don't think the person has told you the entire story.
10. Identity-establishing—Creating the belief that you know the individual; he sets you straight by telling you what you need to know about him.
11. Rapid fire—Asking questions without allowing the person time to answer; as he gets emotional about it, he finally blurts out something. Your intent is to get a piece of incriminating information or a secret, for example.
12. Silence—Using lack of conversation to establish control. You ask a question you know the person does not want to answer and then say nothing more: "What exactly did you say to the client to make her drop us?"

Some approaches require more than one person to pull off so, we coordinate actions. In a meeting, you might adopt the same technique when you have to deliver bad news. One delivers the wound, and one whips out the first-aid kit.

This is one of the many instances where you have a blatant need to specify who must be present at a meeting. Even though it may not be as obvious in other circumstances, this is an important and consistent need. Determine who in the pool can provide relevant information, answer your questions, and help you meet your stated objective.

This process happens at a distance, not as the meeting is taking shape. Spotting your buddy in the hallway and suggesting that she join the meeting on new product development is a bad idea if the gathering is really a meeting. If it's brainstorming over donuts, that's a different thing.

Use the roles that companies put you in to figure out who should and should not get the e-mail invitation to the meeting. Think of it as theater: Certain actors belong on the stage together because of the characters they're portraying, and certain actors have not been cast in this particular play. Depending on your level in the company, the board of directors, some corporate officer, or a supervisor created your role and cast you in it. You're expected to bring your talents and skills, but you aren't expected to change the character from a soldier to a musician.

In the meeting, people's roles are to:

- Answer questions
- Make decisions
- Solve a problem
- Provide functional support (support process)

If you know that Joe Smith can solve a problem, don't invite Joe Jones just because he works in the same department. That's like casting an actor who looks a little like the guy you really want. There is an exception to this: If you think you will be outnumbered or ambushed in a meeting, you might want to bring in people who side with you to fill chairs. In other words, herd your cattle into the pen so that you outnumber the opposition.

The person who provides functional support may be an assistant to the boss who reads people for him, takes notes, keeps track of action items, and gets him to his next meeting on time. Even before you hire someone, your awareness of the kind of people you need in meetings will help you in the interview process. You may need to probe for the ability to multitask or look especially closely to ascertain action style so that the new person fits into your desired team action profile.

After all the planning, it's showtime.

## *Establishing Control*

Once the source enters the interrogation room, the interrogator establishes control by setting some expectations up front. We say things you would never say: "Sit down in *that* chair with your feet flat on the floor and hands on top of your legs and answer questions when you are asked. Don't make any sudden moves." It's part of an up-front contract on participation. You need one as well and the components are detailed in the following sections.

### 1. Time Expectations
- Interview—The amount of time the person will be there is key to creating an expectation and ensuring that you are both aligned. You might push right up to the end asking questions that seem weighty without interest in the answer just to see how he responds. Does his baseline shift? Does he talk faster close toward the end?
- All meetings—Cover the timeline at the beginning of the meeting. It prevents misunderstanding and eliminates a walkout as a pocket veto for discussing the issue.

### 2. Roles
- Interview—Tell the person who everyone in the room is. Explain how the interaction will occur, or not, depending on whether you're trying to stress the interviewee.
- Noninterview meetings—In other meetings the roles should be clearly defined. No one wants to find out you brought a competitor or a government agent to the meeting after it's over.

## 3. Agenda

- Interview—Interviewees like structure. Telling them the interview style up front takes away uncertainty. You want the candidate to know that each of the twelve people on the jury will ask questions at will and to expect cross-examination. By presenting the scenario up front, you will likely keep the interviewee from plunging into full-blown fight or flight if it is his first experience with a murder-board interview.

- Noninterview meetings—Show your agenda to the meeting participants and ask for buy in. Once they've agreed to the agenda, it is difficult not to discuss an issue. Ask them what else and whether the issues are ordered correctly. If they change the order or try to remove an issue, you are prepared for what's coming. If they add an issue and try to take one that you care about off the agenda, make the point of the importance. If the timeline is too ambitious, get agreement about what will be discussed in this meeting, as well as agreement on the next meeting time.

In interrogations, once we have the interviewee's attention, we move to the friendly stuff, that is, rapport building.

## *Rapport Building*

In interrogation, "rapport" means framework for information transfer, not patting each other on the back.

Regardless of whether your encounter is an interview or a regular business meeting, you need to decide on the style of rapport building you intend to use. There are two basic types of rapport: stern and sympathetic. For noninterview meetings, you can chat about off-topic things and run some of the networking ploys like the five questions. For interviews, launch with small talk about how the person found out about your position, and so on.

Take this opportunity to determine a baseline.

Rapport building is the single most neglected step in American business meetings and one that is *key* to determining baseline behavior.

## Approaches

In interrogation, we run approaches after we get the conversation started. They are designed to help us motivate the hostile source if she is anything but a category 1. Typically, you will not need to use approaches in an interview, but you might need an approach in a meeting with an irate customer. That approach might go something like the interchange Mel had with the property management company in Chapter 2, in which the customer had little tolerance for out-risk strategy. By saying to the customer, "We are not as mature as your company in our risk strategy," Mel has run the *pride and ego up* approach discussed previously—along with a healthy dose of deference.

Approaches are rarely used alone, but rather orchestrated with others to create a driver for behavior. In fact, if you notice there is no good cop–bad cop tag team; it is one person orchestrating fear up and the other, fear down. Look through the list and make your own combinations, including those that you would use in collaboration with a colleague. I've used good cop–bad cop by myself and called it "the Ike," in memory of TV depictions of Ike Turner slapping Tina, and then asking, "Why did you make me slap you?" Good interrogation does not involve violence, but manipulation of emotions.

## Questioning

It is in this phase that the interrogator earns her title. She asks questions in quick succession, all the while reinforcing her current approach and reading her source.

In most meetings it is simply the phase where you move from agenda item to agenda item, ensuring that you stick to the script and resolve one issue before moving to another. Or as interrogators would say, "Fully exploit the issue before moving on." If the issue has become bogged and you cannot get past it, use the five questions to change the topic.

## Tools for Interviewing Job Candidates

Job interviews are about finding out if you have a fit for those screening categories you came up with. In effect, your job requirements are identical to PIRs. You need a person who can fit the bill. Ask questions and get answers and you will discover the basic intelligence of the candidate and whether or not he can come up with answers that sound plausible—but that's all you get. But configure the interview so that you force the person to respond under some stress, and you find out what you really need to know. Is he the right person to run a team of people who are difficult? Can she apply her expertise and experience in a high-pressure environment? Tools to get that information—most of which you have already—are:

1. The ability to question like a polygrapher
2. Approaches
3. Elicitation techniques
4. In-depth knowledge about the job

There are few other tools you need to be a good *personality behavioral interrogator:*

• Lead sheets

In an interrogation we prioritize leads as hot or cold. A hot lead gets exploited immediately. If the interrogator is asking about the floor plan of a given building and the source answers, "I have not been there since the spill. I am not that gutsy," then the topic shifts to the hot lead. But if he says, "Yeah, the last time I was in that building, I saw Colonel Jones," Colonel Jones becomes a cold lead, that is, something that the interrogator jots a note about to exploit later.

• Minimizing

Make the consequences of the issue seem less than they really are. In the interrogation world, we might say, "Come on, tell me what you did. We have all made mistakes. Taking cash is no different from a kid stealing candy. It's all the same."

• Eye movement

I find this tool invaluable during an interview. The concept is simple, but mastery of it takes time.

Recognizing a person's pattern of eye movement is part of the baselining process. When remembering something visual, such as how many steps are on the Lincoln Memorial, the person looks up above the brow line. Control questions enable you to determine whether the person's eyes go to the right or to the left for memory. The eyes will go to the opposite side when the person is creating visual details, but the movement will still be above the brow ridge. Your baseline question needs to be only visual, not a complicated question involving multiple senses like, "What was that Lady Gaga concert like?" You also need to make it one that requires thought. A good example is, "You drove through the worst of the traffic today. Where was the biggest bottleneck?"

To determine the auditory cue, do the same thing with a detailed control around something heard. Ask if she listened to the news on the way to work or can remember how a particular song goes. Very likely, the eyes will drift slightly up but stay between the cheekbone and brow line—right around the ear. If you want a contrived example to use as an experiment on your friends, ask them what the fifth word of "The Star Spangled Banner" is. Once you know where they go for memory, you know the opposite side is creative.

No one ever goes to one side for visual memory and the other for auditory memory. Both visual and auditory memories are stored on the same side.

There are only two absolutes when it comes to eye movement. People look down and to the right when they discuss emotional issues and down and to the left when they carry on inner conversations or calculate.

Bringing this full tool suite to bear, you are ready to interview candidates.

## Behavioral Interview Technique Enhanced (BITE)

This four-step process involves asking nontraditional questions, looking for leads, prioritizing leads, asking follow-up questions, and repeating the process. I designed this version of the behavior-based interview technique with certain enhancements related to your need in business to ascertain action style and personality issues. Like any other interview, you need to ensure that the questions you ask do not lead to discrimination. This tool enhances your understanding of the person, rather than zeroing in on the person's experience. Traditional tools can be used to determine whether the person has the experience you are looking for.

One tool is not exclusive of the other, because you need to know about the person's experience as well. Not only can you use both, but you should. Using BITE gives you more of a conversation than a Q&A—just like a good interrogation. It builds on the questioning style covered in Chapter 2 on polygraphers.

Start with PIRs, that is, the primary driver you are seeking. In some fields, you want a warm body because the skills are so rare, and the personality type may be less important because the individual spends all day in a locked laboratory. In that case, direct, traditional questioning works best. When you want information about action style, hot buttons, and how well the person is likely to fit with a team, the BITE style works best. Notice I am talking specifically about action style. Moving the questioning to disposition (selfish versus altruistic; individualistic versus collectivist) is a talent you will need to hone, or you might stray into the person's political ideology—and that is *not* a topic of discussion in job interviews.

**Step 1** Ask a nontraditional interview question that requires the person to actually use cognition and answer with something other than memory.

*Example:* "How do you define yourself?"

You know you have the right kind of question when her eyes go down and to her left as she has an inner conversation. Typically, these nontraditional questions evoke responses that use words filled with connotation and give you room to explore inside the head of the interviewee.

**Step 2** Listen to the actual answer for a lead. Because of the unusual nature of the answers, the body language associated with any part of the answer, or emphasis placed on given words, also gives you big clues as to the type of person you're interviewing.

*Example:* She answers, "Courageous, dedicated, *smart,* industrious."

You notice she struggles with the word "dedicated," picking her nails for the first time. You also notice she is emphatic about the word "smart" by saying it with a different tone and punctuating it by putting her palm flat on the table.

People who use canned phrases to define themselves—"I'm mission-focused"—may be using them because they hold genuine meaning in their culture. So if the person's career is sales, in the sales professional's culture, the phrase might mean, "I do everything I can to serve my customers," in which case the response is a good one.

**Step 3**   Use follow-up questions as you look for understanding of the lead. In this case there are two leads: dedicated and smart. You could choose to follow up on "dedicated," making it a hot lead, and keep "smart" as a cold lead, or do the opposite.

A response like "smart" raises a red flag for me. Does she view herself as smart relative to a really stupid group? If I put that person in a pool with really smart people, will she head-butt to prove herself? Will her self-confidence sink because the other people in her group are smarter than she is? In other phases of the interview, I would deliberately try to find out more about the way she sees herself in relation to other people so that I would know the answers to those questions. But for now, let's make this the cold lead and "dedicated" the hot lead.

To exploit the hot lead, I ask a direct question.

*Example:* "What do you mean by 'dedicated'?"

Alternatively you could use an elicitation technique here, such as, "I have read your résumé. You could not have done all of those things without dedication." You would follow that comment with silence. She will likely come back with a thank you and a comment that is filled with leads.

**Step 4**   Look for leads. Whether you use an elicitation technique or a direct question, her response will provide body language information and more lead information.

Probe the issue of dedication by relying on your common sense. She is struggling with that word for a reason, and it may be the same reason that prompts you to ask: "How does your dedication reconcile with the fact that you're interviewing for a job with a competitor?" As she responds, she will help you to understand what she means and likely open another door into her mind.

The Q&A may play out like this:

Q: "What do you mean by 'dedicated'?"
A: "I work diligently and give my all."
Q: "How is that consistent with your desire to leave?"

This is using the direct question as elicitation. You tie mild criticism into the form of a question. By doing that, you force her to answer the question in a way that defends her choice of words. Along the way she will give you an answer as well as another opportunity to see how she handles stress and direct conflict, how quickly she thinks, and other key traits. You've set it up so that she is in direct conflict with her potential employer—that's stressful. If not handled effectively, you have the likelihood of long-term baggage. However, if you do it correctly, it allows you to see deviation from her baseline in response to stress and how far she is pushed by simple confrontation.

The double-edged question is this:

Q: "How can you use the word 'dedicated' when you are here interviewing with a competitor?"
A: "This looks like a good opportunity, and I am not taking anything away from my company. This is my own time."

That's a solid response, and in it, you see your next lead: She crosses her hands when she says "opportunity." A barrier is the invitation for microinterview. Should you take the invitation or transition to another topic? You might want to know immediately why "opportunity" is an emotionally charged word for her. Usually, this concept evokes positive responses; in this case, she responded with a barrier.

Use direct questions to open the microinterview.

Q: "Is opportunity your driver?" (Fully realizing this can be a negative question, you watch for her to interpret your intent.

She answers quickly and without any eye movement to indicate inner voice.)

A: "Yes, in fact, it's how I define courageous. I do not like to be stagnant." (She raises her palms to punctuate the word "stagnant.")

Now is an opportunity to switch from pure behavior-based questioning back to the traditional tell-me questions, such as, "Tell me about the best opportunity you have ever had." You could also continue with the BITE style. Let's say you choose the latter.

Ask a parallel path question that you suspect will get her to tell you how she thinks:

Q: "What do you like best about your current job?"

A: "The day-to-day work, the hands-on assistance I give customers.

Q: "What do you dislike?"

A: "The lack of opportunity and the stagnation. I have been in the same job for five years."

Now you can use that criticism and direct questioning again to get to her action style:

Q: "What have you done about that?"

A: "Interviewed outside the company. There is nothing else I can do. The system is broken and . . ."

You have your answer: She is a revolutionary. Now, you need to decide whether or not she fits your needs. If the answer is yes, you can go to traditional questions around the skills she has, the systems she knows, and so on. Most important, you have her core type and some understanding of what drives her. If you decide to hire her, you know her impatience is tied up in movement and she will need to have hope restored. You also know you need to instill trust in your system from the beginning. As you understand her fit to your other requirements, you can better make your decision.

You might get this information though traditional interviewing, but the steps would be longer and you would need much more intuition than you do with this behavioral technique. When you use it, you interview like an interrogator.

Pay very close attention to the person. Realize how quickly she catches on that you are probing for behavior. It is a very good sign of how intelligent the person is in terms of interpersonal skills. As you push, remember that you can damage a relationship if you go too far. But give yourself permission to ask what you want to know, either through direct questions or elicitation using the skills you learned in Chapter 3 on networking like a spy.

## Tools of Termination

In interrogations, interim terminations occur anytime we need to take a break, like reporting that the enemy has a planned raid impending. In that case, we reinforce the approach that's working and come up with a logical reason to leave the room. In effect, we use positive reinforcement for what is working, typically allowing just enough time to pass to prevent our running out of the room with the data from looking like a victory dance. Take a lesson from that.

Interim terminations often occur within the meeting when a decision is made or an agenda item is shelved. If a decision is made, you make a clear break between one topic and the next, but you also do a wrap-up and make it clear what the homework is: "Great! We will move forward with the electronic press kit. Sally will take the lead on drafting it. Let's all have comments ready for Sally by the next meeting." If the item needs to be shelved, announce why—"We don't have the people here who can handle this, so let's schedule another meeting in three weeks and make sure they're here. Who are those people?" You need to reinforce the people side of the meeting as you are assigning tasks; be careful not to undermine the approaches that have worked.

### *Mechanics of Termination*

In an interrogation, we terminate for one of the reasons the field manual lists so succinctly:

- The source remains uncooperative throughout the approach phase.
- Either the source or the interrogator becomes physically or mentally unable to continue.
- All pertinent information has been obtained from the source.
- The source possesses too much pertinent information for all of it to be exploited during the interrogation session.
- Information possessed by the source is of such value that his immediate evacuation to the next echelon is required.
- The interrogator's presence is required elsewhere.
- The interrogator loses control of the interrogation and cannot recover it.

This list applies to business meetings just as well.

Interrogators remind the source what they have talked about and that he needs to check it to find out if it is true. He also reminds the source that the information might have some gaps and they might need to talk again. If there were things the source couldn't remember, he gives the source homework to think about those details.

The single most important thing the interrogator does is reinforce what worked. He might loop back to the question about family and revisit the approach, And if he made a promise to get the source a pen and paper to write home, he reinforces that.

## Process for Meetings

Go through the wrap-up and homework process. Before you turn the lights off in the room, you also want to go back into rapport building. If you're meeting with a customer, you might say, "Thanks for bringing me to your facility. It was great to be on site so I could meet some of the other people on your team." And then, if one of your approaches clued you into the fact that this guy was not in a position to make a crucial decision, bring that issue to some resolution: "Glad we could get the conversation started about renewing the contract. I appreciate your willingness to escalate this; please let me know what other information I can give you to help in that process."

At the end of the meeting, you need a sense of resolve and next steps. You don't want the meeting to be over because one person says, "Gotta run!" and another hits the off switch on the LCD projector.

## Process for Interviews

Regardless of whether you plan to hire or not, reinforce the approach that worked to get the applicant talking. Tell her how much the opportunity to meet meant. Let her know the next steps, and how you will be in touch. Treat her as a valuable source that you or someone else might need this time or in the future.

## Turning Around a Bad Meeting

Sometimes meetings go off track, whether from the outset or during the actual conduct. There is a process to turn them around.

First, there are two main reasons why bad meetings occur:

1. You hold them out of habit. That's the mentality of "it's Thursday at 3 o'clock so the committee on paper clips has to meet." The way to turn around that bad meeting is to cancel it. Conduct routine business by following a schedule of e-mail exchanges. There is an important caveat here: You might have to have members of your team put a standing meeting on their calendars so they block out the time to participate if a meeting becomes necessary. You can still cancel it if there's nothing of substance to address. This is not the same as the annoying phenomenon of people who insist on having meetings just because it's Thursday at 3. They are the ones who use meetings as a passive-aggressive control mechanism. They call the meetings because they can.
2. The person conducting the meeting has bad habits.

I had a boss who enjoyed pinning his staff down and watching them twitch. He contradicted, countered, and poked holes in whatever people said. Ostensibly, he did it to force people to a higher level of preparation, but the process got old quickly. When people would ask me about my schedule and a meeting with that guy was on my calendar, I'd just say, "It's an opposite day," and be prepared to defend every word. Sometimes it is a personality issue and the individual has been rewarded to the point; you cannot change the behavior. You can choose to just leave or take a tough stance.

In the case of the attacker, you can prepare much more information than he ever could want and bog him down in details. Or lead with less than he expects, the whole time prepared for exactly what he wants—in effect, sandbagging and then overdelivering in the same meeting. Do this a few times, and you find you have created a pattern that doesn't reward the behavior, that is, assuming you don't get fired in the process. I learned this technique from Special Forces guys who would say "71 is gravy." The reference point was that 70 was a passing grade on various tests. By that phrase, they meant no matter how much they knew, they rarely exposed all of it. They showed just what they needed to show to get the job done. The silent professionals indeed.

You can often avert a bad meeting, or turn one around that's run off course, if you have clarity on how you want to be seen by others in the meeting and how they see you when you walk through the door.

Consider a scenario in which all of the pieces are in place for a horrible meeting: You go in to talk to the information technology (IT) manager about a project that isn't going well. He's used to being beaten up for missing deadlines in delivering projects. You represent the side of the business that controls the funding and brings down the hammer when a project misses the mark.

How he sees you at the outset of the meeting reflects your actual position in the company. The other part is how that position relates to him personally. You could be his boss, a peer his boss uses in an enforcer role, or his boss's equal.

How you want to be seen depends on whether you want to serve as an interpreter between parties in conflict, build a coalition, or dominate the meeting as an enforcer. As a reminder—and I want to avoid saying this in too many places in the book—all three options bring in the ability to question, negotiate, network, and the other skill suites covered in this book. These techniques do not serve you well if used in isolation.

In the early days of working with a large manufacturing company, "Walt" had the same corporate status as my boss. Walt was responsible for all systems globally, but my thumbprints had to be on his budget before he could spend it. We had a lot of baggage going into almost any conversation, particularly because we would be at odds periodically on funding requests. In addition, he was the one blamed when customers weren't happy, but ironically, it was my side of the house that often caused the delivery problems his team had to cope with. It usually came down to people on my end not scoping out the project properly, so he didn't have the parts he needed for an installation. In essence, it was tough for Walt to ever see me as the good guy in a meeting.

Step back from this specific situation and see the different ways it could have played out.

**Interpreter** This distrust between Walt and me is typical of inter-departmental turf wars; everybody points fingers at everybody else.

Department X feels it isn't getting the right information from department A; department A thinks that department X is incompetent. Sometimes they're both right. Department X ends up being incompetent because they don't get the detail they need to do their job well. The problem is that no one stands in the middle translating for both.

And so, one role that the representative of department A could fill is that of interpreter.

Interpret means decode. On one side of the table, you have someone embracing concepts and nomenclature that mean something specific. On the other side, those same ideas and words mean something else. Your job is to clarify, but to do that while sticking to the point of the conversation. If the IT guru talks about the new computer system in terms of delight and superior performance, you may have to interpret that in terms such as "ease of use" and "competitive advantage."

I was a good Arabic linguist, and I'm proud of that. I stood out because I made every effort to communicate even if it embarrassed me. During Operation Desert Storm, we needed tools to build and repair things. The Army had taught me words so that I could negotiate a treaty, but I did not know the words for pliers and pipe wrench. I sucked it up and decided I didn't mind looking stupid as I asked, "Do you have some of that stuff you put on electric wires when you connect them to protect yourself from electricity?" The young Arab squinted his eyes and asked, "Do you mean 'tape'?" Other Army linguists around me felt too stupid to say the same thing—but I got the tape. That's how an interpreter works. A linguist knows the language, but an interpreter cares enough about communication to use it.

As an interpreter, my focus could have been on putting Walt's issues into language that my business unit understood and valued and communicating their issues in a way that Walt saw them as priorities.

**Coalition Builder**   "Walt, the project is falling apart. Tell me what I need to know on my end to help get past the problems." If I begin with that, I come across as a coalition builder. This is the process that King Solomon perfected; it is about aligning arrows for success. Most conflicts start from the idea that what you want and what I want are two different things.

Solomon had two women claiming the same child. His brilliant answer was to decide each woman would get half. In his wisdom, he knew no mother would allow that to happen. When the mother said she would let the other woman have the child, he knew the right answer.

This is common sense application, meaning that when you think any person is trying to sabotage the project, look for the reason and then find ways to make your successes line up. And if you do it as adeptly as Solomon, you cannot lose.

**Enforcer**   Become the enemy like my old commander who drew us together against him. Others will draw together if only to overcome you.

The interrogation cycle and the meeting cycle are the same, starting with "Why do this?" They continue to match up in terms of bringing in the right group to attend the meeting and preparing for the meeting while thinking about every aspect of people, place, process, and timeline. The area where they diverge is around the purpose. An interrogation is two or more people in a contrived environment, with one trying to extract information from the other. Interrogations and interviews share that as the purpose. A key similarity between interrogations and meetings is that, once you start the meeting, someone is in charge whether you appoint him or not. And in all of these encounters, through effective planning and execution, you set yourself up to get what you want efficiently.

CHAPTER 5

# Close a Deal Like a Hostage Negotiator

## Tools
- Managing change
- Taking control
- Overcoming objections
- Reading body language in negotiation

**Your four rules are:**

1. Nobody negotiates well from a position of weakness. Know what the other guy has to lose. As a corollary, you have to be ready to go to conflict when you begin negotiations.
2. Nothing you do in a negotiation strays from the main intent; that is, bend your target to your will. This is all about getting what you want in the most efficient and effective manner possible.
3. You have to create an environment in which the person feels he has a chance to win, even when he doesn't. The only reason anyone negotiates is because he thinks he can win.
4. Sometimes the reason or what he stands to win is not obvious.

Depending on the given situation, people can move from one action style to the other at any time. Hostage takers are revolutionaries filled with passion, and regardless of whether they are artifact or icon thinkers, they have moved to the far extreme of the chart because of that passion. The cause could be anything, very large or very small: ideology, persona, a bad decision, or simply a last-straw annoyance like "someone took my stapler again." Hostage takers have lost all trust in the system, have no hope, and are driven by passion to take out an insurance policy.

The hostage negotiator has one task: to try to restore the person's trust in *something* in order to establish a glimmer of hope and reduce the passion level of the person. Often, hostage takers are in full fight or flight and simply see the hostage as a movable barrier; others do it from ideology to illustrate their point to the system. The negotiator has to uncover the motivation.

## Value to Business

Most of the time, you are not dealing with hostage takers in business, figuratively or literally. There are exceptions when someone realizes she can hold you hostage with a decision, and those exceptions are often created by the hostage herself. Any business depends on closing a deal. That deal can be life or death for your company, and you don't want anyone sitting in negotiation thinking, "I'd rather be shot dead than spend ten more minutes in a room with this guy." You may be holding her hostage with your presentation, but she is holding you hostage by withholding a decision on the deal.

You also don't want anyone concluding that she has nothing to gain by negotiating with you—nothing to win and nothing to lose by walking away.

Fundamentally, what you're doing in a negotiation is managing change. You are driving someone toward a realization that whatever happens next may be very different from what she originally envisioned, but the outcome is her decision. It reflects her plan. It's what she wants and what's good for her. You are simply there to make it all happen.

You do this through the process of bonding and differentiating. You bond someone to you by helping the person feel special or solving a point of pain. In other words, she feels differentiated from others in her environment. You do this by creating a new reality.

# Tools of Negotiating

Hostage negotiators essentially take a person who is in a high state of revolutionary and move him toward the opposite extreme. In effect, a hostage taker moves into the situation, isolates everything from the outside world, creates a microcosm that he owns, and reestablishes faith and hope in that artificial world. They create a bond that makes the hostage taker become someone who trusts in the system on a micro level; that is, he learns to trust the negotiator. To do this, the negotiator needs these basics:

- An overall understanding of human nature
- A grasp of the situation
- An understanding of the individual he is dealing with
- The audacity to use his assessment of the person
- Tools for moving the action style of the hostage taker

## *Managing Change*

As I said, negotiation is fundamentally change management, so all of these steps apply to you.

**Overall Understanding of Human Nature**   Negotiators typically do not attend a school for negotiators, but rather learn the task through experience. This doesn't mean they stride into a hostage situation and pick up a bullhorn never having done anything like it before. It means that, through years of working in law enforcement, they learn about the psyche of people who take hostages. If you ask many police officers to teach you the things in this book, they can't do it, but they can and do use them. The nature of dealing with people in any given situation teaches you how to think like and deal with those people.

An old analyst I once knew who had been in Vietnam and seen many interrogations would often say that interrogators are the bastard cousins of the prisoner. He meant that our psyches were locked in a dance, making us think and act more like the prisoners than our fellow soldiers. The same is true with law enforcement—and in many businesses with providers and customers.

Give yourself credit for what you know about human nature as it pertains to your business, such as knowing how your customers think. If you have a vacuum about your customers' psyches, fill that vacuum; don't simply continue to wonder. You also know a lot more about human motivation after the first set of chapters than most people. Even though I have spent decades studying people, you likely have a better understanding of your customers' thinking than I could get quickly. You focus squarely on their needs and have created a reasonably good image of what a person who needs what you sell is like.

**Grasp of the Situation**  When a negotiator gets on the scene, he wants to know everything about the situation. Often when he arrives, he gets a situation report (SITREP) delivered by the officer or agent in charge. This includes everything known, including information on the suspect, hostages, and demands, as well as timelines, floor plans, friendlies and unfriendlies on site, and past contact.

• Players

Before he starts a conversation, he needs to know whether his asking about any specific item will calm or agitate the hostage taker. Things such as relationships between the parties in the situation and how contact has been made in the past all play into the conversation. If there is more than one hostage taker, he also wants to know which one appears to be in charge and any personality traits or conflicts.

This has key business applications. In understanding who can make the decision, you just need a path to get you to her. Are you currently talking to the right person for the sale, or will you negotiate your way to an endorsement that will get you to the decision maker? Both are valid paths, but they involve different discussions. You also want to be cautious about hot-button issues; know them before you start the conversation. Most of the time, this information comes from people who are on site or those who have had contact with the target in the past. Take advantage of your network to find out who else knows something about the customer.

- Timeline

The timeline for the negotiator is crucial for two primary reasons: Stockholm syndrome and urgency.

1. Stockholm syndrome—When people are in a high-stress situation, they start to emulate their captor. The results are a bonding between the hostages and the captor. Hostages and taker alike often start to identify the cops as a common enemy, as the SERE commander was a common enemy to us; when that happens, they bond even more closely. There is benefit to the negotiator in the hostage taker seeing his captives as people and not widgets.
2. Urgency—How much time is left before the hostage taker makes a move? If the taker has set a timeline, or more important, has a timeline imposed on him, he is likely to make rushed decisions.

Both of these factors play into your timeline as well. Have you earned the trust of the customer to the point you can stage a delay or press forward quickly? If so, this is much easier. Also realize the decision timeline might be a forced issue. He might need a solution sooner rather than later and that fact will shape your choice of how to approach him when using your tools of persuasion.

- Friendlies and unfriendlies

Both play in as well. Do your homework: What does the competition have that you don't? Be prepared to address those issues; put a spotlight on the elephant in the room. Send a message that's a flawed elephant.

- Understanding the individual

It is likely that while en route to the scene, the negotiator has run background checks on the hostage taker and used every source available to get as much information as possible about the taker, including searches on Facebook, MySpace, LinkedIn, Google, and all the other basic web-based tools. She is specifically looking for the levers to move him up the $x$- and $y$-axis of the action matrix.

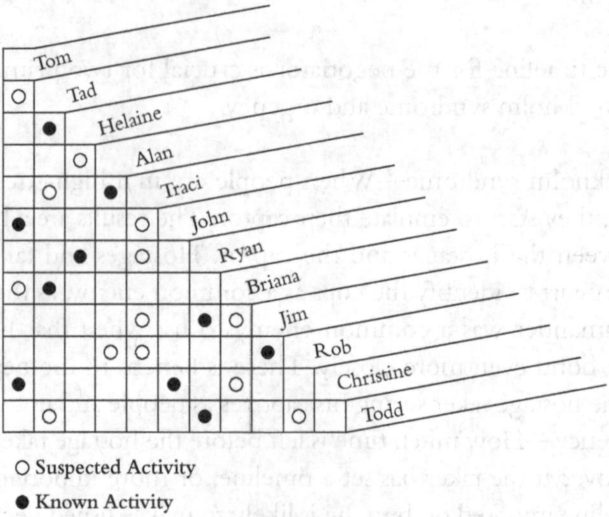

○ Suspected Activity
● Known Activity

FIGURE 5.1   Association Matrix

The association matrix and activities matrix are tools in the intelligence world for linking people to actions and to other people who help as you look for resources that can provide information. I have modified them to suggest how you might use them.

Collect information on your target from both research and observation. If you've already accumulated impressions and information about the person from previous meetings, try to remain objective so that your own filters don't distort your reading of him in the meeting. One of the biggest errors many people make is going into a meeting completely focused on themselves. You won't close a deal by putting your main attention on what you are going to say and do. The customer is one who should command your attention.

The individual's personal life is fair game; you want to know everything that can help you forge a connection and get leverage. You can find out where he lives, whether or not he has kids, and maybe even what clubs he belongs to. All of this most likely falls into the category of basic information, since you have no idea whether or not it will be useful. Collect it anyway.

When the Army gave me an interrogation assignment, I not only read that person's file, I examined everything that had been removed from his pockets. If time allowed, I watched him interact with other people and saw what his normal behavior pattern was.

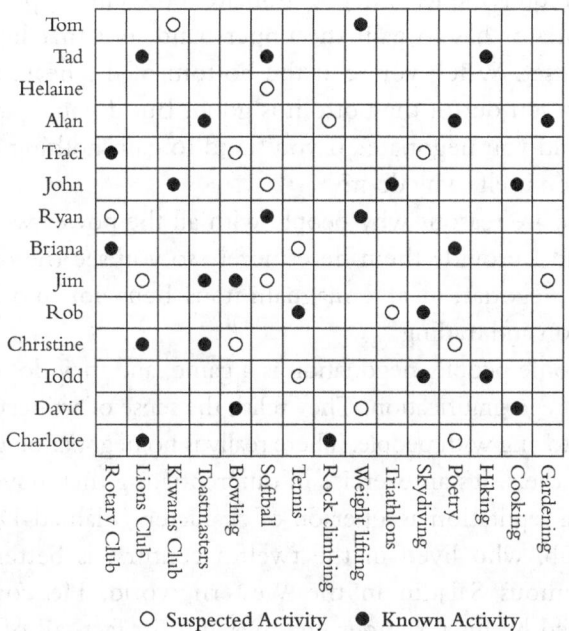

O Suspected Activity    ● Known Activity

**FIGURE 5.2**   Activities Matrix

Doing that gave me clues as to what his deviations from baseline looked like.

In my business life, this level of preparation has served me very well. When I walk into a meeting, I know more about the people I'm meeting with than they know about me. That knowledge is power. It gives me a distinct advantage, regardless of the purpose of the meeting.

Your ability to sort personalities definitely comes into play as you compose your background information. You will take the facts you collected and see what they tell you about the person's character: Do his interests and history suggest he's an altruist who cares about the greater good? Or is he an ego-centered person who plays well on a team? The latter might be someone who has summited Mt. Everest. Everything you know about that person will affect how you approach him. It will guide you in knowing when and how to cause stress and when and how to counter it.

Taken together, the information you collect and behaviors you observe will give you what you need to fast-track establishing rapport.

Think about why he would negotiate.

The requirements of negotiation are rooted in the premise that the negotiator has to gain the upper hand, not that he holds it at the outset. When you're at the bottom of the heap, anything that takes you out of the bottom is good. But if you're at the top, why would you negotiate? If you stand to gain nothing from the negotiation itself, why do it?

There are reasons why people with all the power will "negotiate," and I provide them here merely so you see the difference between negotiation and magnanimous behavior and between negotiation and trading.

For some people, negotiation is a game, and they do it because they want ego gratification. They relish the sense of artificial victory; they like toying with people. There really is no negotiation going on.

For others, it's an exercise in differentiating themselves, a way to build a reputation as a person of character. Salāh ad-Dīn Yūsuf ibn Ayyūb, who lived in the twelfth century, is better known as the famous Saladin in the Western world. He could have been hated by his Crusader enemies and, in fact, all of Europe. Instead, they celebrated him as a chivalrous man. A strict adherent of Sunni Islam, he negotiated magnanimously and earned the respect of allies and enemies as a result of behaving with honor in negotiations—and he consistently had the upper hand in them.

Ulysses S. Grant also negotiated generously just because he felt it was right. As a result, Grant released all the Confederate soldiers in his sight April 1865. He could have put them in prison or shot them. Instead, he let them go home and even let some of them take their hunting rifles.

There is a difference between trading and negotiating, and I use the term "trading" as a euphemism for bullying. When the Romans conquered a population and declared, "You can pay us tariff, and then we will let you live" they were not negotiating. They traded safety and citizenship in the Roman Empire for allegiance and money. That's called extortion.

This is how parents often "negotiate": "Your mother can tell you no, or I can tell you no. Which do you want?" In that same vein, one of my mentors at SERE school used to say, "There are two ways to do things: hardly and easily." Hardly meant he would beat the crap out of you until you did it; easily meant you would do it without having him beat the crap out of you.

In situations in which one party has dominance and chooses to exercise it, to pretend a negotiation is occurring is a fallacy. The person in power who wants to discuss acting in a particular way is not negotiating, even though you may feel as though you have won something. You feel better because she gives you some kind of reward afterward. You did it—great! Now have some ice cream. This ingrains a pattern of capitulation in you—that's all. You negotiated nothing. You are becoming Pavlov's dog.

This scenario illustrates pushy behavior, but not bullying: I wanted to buy a computer, but didn't want to pay the price I saw online. I called the company and asked the rep what kind of price he would give me. He quoted the same price I saw online. I said, "You just went online and ran the same set of specs I did to come up with that, didn't you?"

"Yes."

"Why do you think I called you?" No response. "I called you to get a better deal." No response. "You're afraid of losing a piece of your commission, aren't you?"

"Yes."

"Well if you don't give me a better deal, your commission is my dial tone."

"You mean you're going to hang up on me?" he asked.

"Yes." And then I got a better deal.

Know what you want when you start a negotiation. The minute I'm at "nothing to lose," every move is a positive one. If the computer cost $1,890 and he brings it down to $1,840, I saved $50 just by talking. If I save $50 for every 30 seconds I talk, that's not bad.

Axiom: A person with nothing to lose has everything to gain. He needs to understand that.

**Audacity to Do the Job** Audacity is a learned skill set for all intelligence collectors and people in law enforcement—and it's required. In any of those professions, you have to be prepared to give yourself the liberty to fail. There are times when you will make a mistake and someone's life is on the line. You have to compartmentalize, and tell yourself you were the best person for the job even if you fail.

Audacity does not mean tough talk and "won't take no for an answer," as in the stereotypical used-car salesman's approach. That guy would definitely get the hostages killed—or kill the chance of closing a big deal. You develop audacity as you refine your ability to influence human behavior to get the outcome you desire. You rarely get the desired outcome when the "negotiator" is the human equivalent of a jackhammer.

Once the negotiator arrives on site, he takes control and begins to use what's in his toolbox. He first and foremost needs absolute control of the situation to create a sense of trust. In effect, what he is doing is creating a microcosm in which he is the system and the system engenders trust in our revolutionary.

You do the same in business, creating a sense of trust in what you can deliver and hope that you are the right person.

## Taking Control

You want the hostage taker to bond with you. Principally, you do that by convincing him you can do something for him and that you will do it. When a negotiator takes control, it is not a euphemism. It means he owns the operation. He controls all communication with the suspect. He decides what the taker and hostages get to eat and drink and whether the phones work. He is creating a model of ownership. With use of these tactics, he is creating an alternative world—one that makes the taker believe that he has the power to make all decisions. As a control tactic, negotiators configure a situation in which the hostage taker is forced to bond with the hostages. The negotiator might say, "I'm shutting off your electricity, and after you tell me where your hostages are— one by one—I'll turn it back on." Getting him to do that is part of inching toward control, but it also serves the purpose of forcing him to speak to the hostages. Maybe he even discovers someone from his home town. As the hostage taker capitulates with small demands from the negotiator, he is rewarded to establish trust. The negotiator stalls through the use of techniques like "I don't have the authority to do that. I will need a couple of hours to get you an answer." He stalls through the use of negotiation on unimportant points to take control of the taker's timeline and turn it into his own. This should sound familiar to you because you learned to negotiate agenda in Chapter 4 on interviewing like an interrogator. Each decision he takes away from the taker is creating a conditioned response, all the while balancing getting cooperation with engendering trust and creating hope.

## Taking Control in Business

Using tools from the interrogator section, establish control of the room to create a microcosm. Make it clear, "This meeting is all that matters for the next 90 minutes."

The real driver is the opportunity to get trust from the customer, not to present cold, hard facts, but to move her into the position of seeing your product as an extension of you in delivering hope and trust.

Bond through rapport building to obtain common ground.

Use the tools you know—five questions, common ground, and elicitation—to get closer. If you have common allies, the two of you should "discover" that as well.

Start the meeting by ensuring she buys into your agenda. Make it a negotiation point early to get her to contribute, and then negotiate order logically. Create a reason for her to negotiate with you—one that has only one logical outcome and then practice it.

## Negotiate

You work your way into the agenda and the first point of negotiation arises. You need to decide how this should be handled: Do you want to win or problem solve?

You need to know the answer to that question before you start. Just as in the hostage situation, some things are not negotiable. Know which ones are and which ones aren't. Like Mel in the terms-and-conditions story in Chapter 2, know how flexible you can be. You can make a decision whether you need to train the customer to say yes on this point, or you can appear magnanimous and gain trust by solving the customer's problem. Only through controlling your own emotions and paying attention to his can you effectively negotiate.

• Use an assistant to maintain control.

While the negotiator works his magic, an assistant can observe, take notes, and report. If the negotiator's ego starts to rise up, or he misses something the target said, the assistant can give immediate input. The nature of human interaction makes it easy for chemistry to take hold and people to get lost in the conversation. A person charged with remaining out of the action and just paying attention can provide invaluable, timely insights.

- Do what it takes to stay out of fight or flight.

The negotiator's control depends on both parties staying far from a high-stress fight-or-flight condition. The negotiator has to appear to care about the person but, at the same time, must remain detached so that he can methodically get the hostage taker to be more compliant. He will never be compliant if he's terrified and in a state of fight or flight. If a contract negotiator for your company makes a customer feel profoundly uncomfortable, you may get a nod on the spot only to realize later that there's no ink on the page. Remember: This is all about engendering trust to create a belief that you can solve his problem.

## Overcoming Objections

Your three primary techniques are to trigger an epiphany, minimize the problems, and unbundle the argument.

**Trigger an Epiphany** The bad guy demands an airplane. The negotiator approaches the request logically: "Do you really think an airplane can land in this little parking lot?"

The hostage taker now asks for a getaway car.

The negotiator continues on a logical and consistently helpful track: "How will that help you?"

"I will get to the airport."

"And then what?" The negotiator makes the taker see the futility of the request, all the while trying to help and creating a sense of trust.

This concept is important in all parts of business, not just contract negotiation, because change management may be the most complex thing we do in business. Getting people to adopt an idea through epiphany, rather than forcing it down their throat, is the way to get people to embrace change. When they can explain, "This is good for me because . . . ," then you have them on your side. It is even better when they have discovered the answer; they don't have to know you helped.

The negotiator may make minor concessions in moving through this process, but those concessions are never about giving the guy an advantage. For example, it wouldn't make sense for the negotiator to send in the bad guy's child so he could spend some nice after-school time with her.

**Minimize the Problems** The negotiator may also use a technique called "minimizing." For example, he might tell the hostage taker that what he did wasn't as bad as what John Doe did last month in Akron.

A common example is when you make a major purchase, such as a house or a car. Since you will no doubt see something wrong with it, even a small thing, the seller needs to know how to minimize that flaw so that you will buy it anyway. When my friend Mimi was planning her move to the Rocky Mountains, she went to the car dealer from whom she'd purchased a car that was great for California highways. The one car on the lot that seemed appropriate for the new environment was a bright yellow, four-wheel drive sport utility vehicle (SUV). Seeing that her repeat customer didn't like the yellow, the sales pro said, "Won't you be in a lot of snow?"

"Yes."

"Then isn't yellow a great color—people will see you in a snowstorm!"

Whether she thought it through or not, she minimized the pain of buying what Mimi thought was an ugly car. Thereafter, if she ever needed an excuse for buying the car, she could recite the logical reason that it was easy to see in a snowstorm. Minimizing is a way to let a person feel good about making a mistake. When you give someone permission, he trusts you because he feels as though you are looking out for his good.

The alternative to success in a negotiation is harsh. In a hostage situation, the guy who thinks he has no ability to dictate terms and no way out will conclude: "I'm either gonna die from a bullet or walk out of here with handcuffs, so I might as well kill the hostages."

You know the equivalent in business, whether you sell product or any kind of services, including professional services. Give the person no options and you have no deal—no matter how much it will benefit him or his company.

**Unbundle the Argument**   You can also do that by convincing him that he makes no sense. For example, I had an employee who wasn't very good at math. He came in to negotiate a salary increase and asked for $1/hour more. I pushed back; that's $2,000 a year and I didn't want to give it to him. When I told him no, he said he wanted 25 cents more an hour "or else." "Or else what?" I asked him.

"I'll quit!"

I said, "You mean you're going to quit your job for $10 a week?" When he thought about it in those terms, he put his tail between his legs and went away.

Sometimes negotiation is that simple because the person you're talking to is not rational. In a hostage negotiation situation, or in business, that will happen if the person enters into a state of fight or flight, which I explored in Chapter 2. At that point, he has lost cognitive ability and moved into a state where animal impulses start to dominate.

In the business world, a common scenario is that you encounter someone who is having a hard time making a decision. You need to strengthen the bond as you overcome objections. One by one, you want to take out those objections, break them down, and overcome them.

Interrogators and spies do exactly the same thing: slowly remove objections. Grind away at them until they become a barely noticeable smudge. Much of the time, people's objections are more emotion than fact. So if you can point out that the underpinnings of the objection are flawed, then the arguments themselves are flawed. If it can be done in a hostage situation, it can absolutely be done in a business meeting.

## Reading Body Language in Negotiation

You've already seen how reading body language to detect stress and possible deception aids in questioning, but reading body language in negotiation requires special focus on acceptance or rejection. You are setting up a circumstance in which establishing trust is essential. You need to see the signs of success or failure.

**Body Language of Acceptance**   When you are winning someone over in a negotiation, the body language bleeds acceptance.

Among other behaviors that show openness and deference, the person will:

- Mirror your movements
- Raise the chin up to your level such that the chin is not protecting the throat
- Keep the chin level even with you, not raised higher in indignation
- Stay engaged with the eyes; the eyes might drift off to imagine possibilities (remember the eye movement cues in the section on interrogation)
- Smile slightly
- Start to soften body movements while internalizing what you're saying

**Body Language of Rejection** Conversely, when you have pushed too hard or simply not struck a chord with the person in the negotiation, you will see some or all of these signs:

- Increased barrier use to increase the separation between you
- Chin raised high in indignation or positioned slightly down
- Avoidance of eye contact
- Use of adaptors, signaling nervousness
- Change of pitch or cadence

An extremely negative response will include overt symptoms of fight or flight.

You might also see the person's coping mechanism surface. It's a kind of "superadaptor" to help a person relax in a very taxing situation. Some coping mechanisms are positive ways of releasing energy; some are negative. You need to know what yours is so that you can prevent it from surfacing during a negotiation or meeting and consequently causing a disruption.

I had someone on a team who giggled when she felt stress. I had to train her out of it and help her find some other way of coping because the giggling made her seem unprofessional and got on people's nerves. Some people cope by acting harsh. If you're in a tense negotiation with a customer, his nervousness about not having control might leak out as a sarcastic attack. He would be sending a dramatically wrong message about his state of mind.

Some behaviors are taught. Coping mechanisms are no different. You do what works, and if no one takes offense, or if they reward you for it by easing up on the stress, then you will repeat it. Even if a coping mechanism is negatively judged by external sources, it may still be positively rewarded by the ego. On the other hand, like most behaviors, coping mechanisms will disappear if they aren't rewarded or if they are punished when they first show up.

The tools negotiators use are based on simple human motivators, such as those captured in Maslow's Hierarchy of Needs. While they talk about things like trust and hope to the hostage taker, they are not talking to him about "why." When faced with a person who has lost all trust, they take control of the environment to establish a new reality, one in which they are the system and need to be trusted. By moving the three axes of the action matrix, they affect the person's action style and convert him into a person who wants to play by the rules of that new reality. Since you know you can change action styles of a person by managing trust, hope, and passion, they are the levers for your negotiation. Create an environment of trusting you to provide what the other person needs and hope you will get better outcomes.

CHAPTER 6

# Research Like
# an Analyst

## Tools
- Identifying gaps
- Targeting research
- Determining sources
- Transferring information
- Vetting sources
- Calculating proximate reality
- Matching audience and packaging

There are multiple types of analysts within intelligence organizations. Rather than spend a tremendous amount of time on the types, I want to talk about some of the things they do. Specifically:

1. Collection management
2. Collection support
3. Single-source analysis
4. All-source analysis

These four groups might seem redundant until you understand how they function. Collection managers are just that: They tell the collectors—people like me in the field—what to collect. Then we trudge off to do it. But it is not just human intelligence (HUMINT) gatherers like me; it is also:

147

- Image intelligence (IMINT)
- Open-source intelligence (OSINT)
- Photo intelligence (PHOTINT)
- Signal intelligence (SIGINT)

We have words for each of the types, and most are derogatory things like "squint" for imagery analysts and "antenna heads" for SIGINT. I am sure they have names for us, too, but they are afraid to tell us.

Analysts do four primary things: task collectors, support collectors, analyze information, and brief intelligence. Analysts are the guts of the intelligence system, or as my old friend Mr. Stewart said, "Analysts drive the train." They look at the intelligence picture, decide where there are gaps, and tell us what we need to collect. They read our reports, verify whether the information is real or not, and add it to the intelligence picture.

On a regular basis, they are taking our ingredients and making sausage. The kinds of sausage they make are targeting details for air raids, hostage rescue missions, and just about anything needed by the bill payers (for example, infantry). The audience depends on the analysts' assignment and mission.

Analysts for the CIA create daily briefings for the president. The Presidential Daily Brief is clearly a strategic document. At the tactical level, they are telling the hostage rescuers where the escape hatch is on the roof and the thickness of the roof. They take highly sensitive information, look for holes, cut those holes into discrete packages, and ask us to find what belongs there. They turn our garbage into actionable intelligence, and then report it out.

Analysts with the CIA know their audience is the president of the United States, who needs the information to make decisions regarding international relations. Priority information answers as many of the basic interrogatives as possible: who, what, when, where, why, and how. Reliable sources can include individual people, open sources, signal and imaging technology, and photographs. In most cases, they are dealing with incomplete information, which means they have to take it and connect the dots to create as close to a complete and accurate picture as possible. Finally, they prepare the package for the president and are sensitive to how the president prefers to have the information. For example, in addition to hearing and reading the Presidential Daily Brief on intelligence issues, George H.W. Bush liked to have portions of the briefing on index cards so that he could review them later when he had the chance. And on occasion, the intelligence services would supplement the briefing for Ronald Reagan with short videos.

All good analysts do one thing very well: They package information in ways that are useful, not spending tremendous amounts of time on extraneous data, but prioritizing what is important and how to deliver it in the most useful way.

## Value to Business

Excellent research is actionable intelligence. It highlights and prioritizes options, points to ways of saving time and money, and provides insights that give decision makers a creative advantage. That creative advantage could translate into any number of things, from a new product line to a solution to a problem that seemed unsolvable. For example, solid research led to Procter & Gamble's development of Swiffer, which now ranks as its second best-selling product. The research illustrated precisely what women (especially American women) ages twenty-five to forty-five would find desirable in a cleaning implement. After that, it was just a matter of getting teams of scientists and designers to create it.

The marketing vice president for a new technology company hired a colleague he'd worked with at Apple Computer to do some consulting work. He had confidence that her industry knowledge and connections would make her market research thorough and reliable. Her report was a tool to help the CEO make critical decisions about taking their product into vertical channels such as law enforcement and construction. So who was her audience? Jean focused on the vice president who had hired her. As a result, the report met his specified requirements and pleased him tremendously. But the package was in the wrong format for the CEO and lacked the visual appeal that he preferred. The company's entire office had the vibrant colors and geometric designs he had personally chosen; he placed almost as much value on presentation style as he did content. Jean didn't lose the contract, but she missed a chance to reinforce her position with the CEO.

The simple fix in this situation was a question: "Mike, do you intend to roll the information from my report into a briefing document for the CEO, or do you want me to prepare this for his eyes?"

It is not at all uncommon for both consultants and staff members to get the requirements for a report and not know the real need behind the request. I have seen permutations of this problem many times—and many times, they are caused by an executive who does not want to reveal his true agenda.

In one instance, the CEO asked his product development team to evaluate a component for possible inclusion into their overall system. They came back with complete specifications on the component and a recommendation that the company license the technology. The CEO asked for a meeting with the inventor; he intended to woo him to the company so that he would design the next generation of his gadget for them—but he didn't tell anyone. He asked for a report about the inventor, but was not specific about why he wanted it. He asked for information about the man's education, prior professional accomplishments, and published works. What he got back was a complete, and very impressive, résumé.

When the CEO walked into the meeting, he was expecting to make a generous offer of employment. Instead, his gut response was, "Oh, no." He saw a fat man who smelled like cigarettes and had his leg up on a chair. The inventor was a 50-year-old egomaniac with myriad health issues related to lifestyle excesses. In terms of thought process and physical presentation, he represented the anti-employee to the CEO. It had already cost the company airfare, hotel, and meals to bring the man from Virginia to their California offices. On top of that, for the next two hours, the CEO politely wasted time in a room with someone he wished would disappear. He wanted the technology, but he definitely did not want the man.

Since the CEO's team could not read his mind, they might have avoided the disaster by suggesting he actually talk to the man over the phone before inviting him to the meeting. They could also make a few suggestions when asked for the report. Things like, "It might help in negotiations if we gave you a better-rounded sense of him—like if he plays golf or tennis."

# Tools of Research

## *Roles in Analysis*

In the CIA, there are armies of analysts with specialties in banking, chemical weapons, probably everything but hairstyles. (I may have to take that back in a second edition after the hairstyle experts flame me.) These people are hired for their industry expertise and are often accomplished in one career before they start the other. There are also experts in political affairs, economics, and so on, for geographic areas, so these people make a career out of specialized research. Although we cannot help you develop that kind of research expertise in five easy lessons, there are parts of what they do that are pertinent to you.

Analysts that I've worked with look at everything we have. All-source analysts, the masters of the battlefield, are the people who update the modern equivalent of the sand table, those small-scale models used for military planning and training: They keep commanders at the theater or local level apprised of what is happening and roll that intelligence up to the national level. Consider the lesson in that model for you in business.

You likely have more in common with the all-source guy trying to understand where a given tidbit fits in the grand scheme of things than a CIA analyst, but you will get a taste of both with a focus not only on research, but also on packaging.

## *Identifying Gaps*

Analysts start with a picture of the known. In the Cold War, that may have been the order of battle holdings that were maintained as a massive database, including the names of every commander in the 43rd Motorized Rifle Regiment or the personality traits of someone like KGB General Oleg Kalugin (now most decidedly a friend of the United States).

Because of their expertise, they can look at that picture and, to some extent, identify what is unknown. They then start the process of making the picture complete.

Analysts mine intelligence to complete the picture. Regardless of where they work, analysts need to be schema thinkers. By that I mean they need to look at the known from time to time and see what has changed. In this way they are like gardeners, constantly managing the health of the intelligence they own.

"What don't we have here?" is a question they would ask.

When analysts discover there is a gap either because we never had the intelligence or because the schema has changed, they immediately set out a plan for how to fill this new gap. They don't simply use intuition and say, "It must be this." They might have a belief, but they validate that belief with fact whenever possible.

When they realize there is missing information, they have to decide where to get it. There are numerous resources, from people to open-source tools to their own classified means. For your purposes, I will focus on human intelligence sources and open-source tools. But before any digging occurs, you need to first understand how the data will be used. After that, your resources can be put to work.

## Targeting Research

This is about who needs it and why. Knowing that, how do you decide what information is most important?

**The Audience**  Think for a minute about a CIA analyst focused on knowledge of financial institutions trafficking terror-related money. Is she briefing SEALs about the bank, or the president of the United States? The mismatch means she could intrinsically pick the wrong level to do her research or target the wrong collectors.

As the story of Jean preparing her report for the wrong person illustrated, you must identify your audience in both conducting the research and packaging it. Having done that, you need to *know* your audience. In Chapter 2, I introduced you to source leads, but I focused on how they surface in conversation. Source leads can be written material and physical objects as well as the spoken word. They can be e-mails, blogs, and Facebook postings. Clothing, handheld gadgets, and cars tell you something, too. If a colleague uses his iPhone to tell time, log calendar information, send messages, take pictures, send Tweets, and watch movies, you can certainly get a conversation started about iPhone apps. And source leads from the spoken word aren't just the words. You can pick up the relative importance of a topic, or something that causes stress, by changes in tone, cadence, pitch, and style of vocabulary.

Those source leads will give you insights into the person's disposition, which may affect what he's likely to view as priority information and may also give you a better grasp of why he needs it. Let's say your audience is a senior executive you might best describe as a cowboy—a selfish individualist—but you count yourself among the Mother Teresa altruistic collectivists. From the start of your research through packaging, keep his disposition in mind, not yours. Later, you will also draw on your knowledge of action styles to help determine how best to package the information.

**Why the Audience Needs the Information** The more specific you are about your requirements, the better.

During the Cuban Missile Crisis of 1962, President John F. Kennedy needed intelligence that would tell him decisively whether or not the Soviet Union had the firepower to beat the United States in a showdown. CIA case officers had forged a relationship with Colonel Oleg Penkovsky, a senior weapons and military affairs expert, so in a report to the president, the CIA gave the president what he needed. Armed with the facts of the Soviet Union's weapons limitations, Kennedy told them to back off.

All too often, requests for research have a vague structure: "Get me information on opening a store in Jefferson City." Okay, am I to presume you want that because you want to open a store there, or because you want to tell the board that it's a stupid idea to open a store there? Employees tasked with research who have no connection to the purpose are not mentally set up to handle the next three steps in the process.

**Priority information** This is the information you must have or your research is worthless. It includes core concepts, news and trends related to the subject, and anchor points for your target audience.

As much as my editors at the publishing houses have warned, "Don't use Wikipedia as a source," I'm here to tell you that Wikipedia is a decent way to pick up core concepts. People who put the entries together tend to know something more than the average person about the subject matter or individual. Wikipedia also has a staff to keep contributors honest. Look at what the authors of these pages have turned into hyperlinks to get a cursory idea of key concepts. For example, I entered "particle radiation" in a Wikipedia search and got five hyperlinked terms up front: atomic nucleus, charged alpha particle, charged beta particle, photon, and neutron. I think it's safe to say these are core concepts. Once you get the framework, you can find absolutely reliable sources. Moreover, easily available sources like people who write on Wikipedia use the names of the real experts and institutions to add credibility to the article. They create a good starting point for you to hound dog the truth.

The way to spotlight them is by knowing the anchor points for the audience. If the analyst has ten bits of priority information for the CEO and his primary concern is the timeline for a project, then don't make him wade through budget data and product specs to get to what he considers the most important intelligence.

## *Determining Sources*

Armed with the certainty of what you need to research and who will consume it, you need to determine your best source(s). Let's first start with the hard way: using collectors. It's the hard way because the minute you introduce people, you introduce all the variables I've covered up to now.

Collectors come in many forms, from interrogators to enemy spies to the other types you read about previously. All have two things in common: reliability and information transfer.

You can look at reliability in two ways: (1) Is it hearsay or first-hand information? and (2) is the actual source of the information reliable? In the case of an interrogator or other collector, the information is filtered through the collector and the source must be vetted in addition to the filter; in the case of another expert, the source must be vetted closely.

Reliability of the Source   I was listening to a serious discussion about the alcoholic beverage law in Pennsylvania and nearly ran off the road when I heard one of the speakers tout his credentials. He actually said he had written a paper on the subject in college. I thought, "If I'd written a paper on female orgasm in college, does that make me an expert?" That isn't good enough. That's expertise-by-affiliation. That makes as much sense as "I live two blocks from Harvard, so I must be smart."

The best analysts are genuine experts.

The CIA hires people with different backgrounds as analysts and then builds on their existing expertise. They hone the skills of the analysis on the job while also exposing them to more information and situations related to their areas of expertise. For example, the Agency would probably send a person whose specialty is Balkan nations to the Balkan nations for a few months and send a person with a background in weapons systems to a facility that makes weapons. The process of analysis also deepens their expertise as they sift through intelligence reports, but they aren't just people who are brilliant at analysis suddenly learning about a subject from documents coming in from the field.

So in the Agency, "research like an analyst" implies that you have substantial background in the information you're analyzing. In business, that may or may not be the case. You might be tasked with an analysis project in marketing simply because you work in the marketing department or have a master's in business administration (MBA).

Although any fellow analyst in the CIA will be a reliable resource because of the rites of passage and process to get that person there, just any old expert you meet might not be so reliable. Whether it is the person you work with, or a certified expert, you have to be professionally suspicious.

**Reliability of Substance** When a supposed expert cannot give a straight answer to a straight question in her area of expertise, she's covering up for a hole in her knowledge. She may be the right person to conduct the research, but you may not want her to unless she comes clear about her limitations.

To a great extent, research requires having enough of a grasp on the subject to recognize important surprises. In other words, if you have limited understanding of a subject, your focus will tend to be narrow; you'll look for information that seems familiar. If you have deep familiarity with a subject, you see windows where less knowledgeable people see walls.

In many environments, IT personnel have gotten away with having gaps in their knowledge because everyone else treated them like they had mojo. Those people with Birkenstocks and shorts controlled the obscure information that made the systems hum; so what if they're a little weird: They know *everything* about computers.

Use the questioning skills in Chapter 2 to help you discern between a genuine expert and a wannabe.

## Transferring Information

Good analysts categorize what they want collected so that they do not get the interrogator's toy box back. In fact, most interrogators in my time started off learning to do what is called order of battle (OB) interrogations. The OB interrogation was built around Army units and provided superb training for all aspects of questioning; it also created onerous reporting requirements.

This methodical way of establishing factors to shape collection and reporting meant that when the small-chunk analyst wanted information about the large-chunk interrogator's information, it was clearly structured in the report in their way. The analyst was both questioner and interpreter.

Some of these factors lend themselves to business nicely.

- Composition—structure of the organization
- Disposition—where resources are deployed
- Strength—numbers we face
- Tactics and operations
- Training
- Logistics support—how and how well supplied and resupplied
- Combat effectivenes—steel on target, current troop strengths, etc.
- Electronic technical data
- Personalities
- Miscellaneous data

With use of this set of categories, the information is easily retrieved and usable; otherwise, the consumers of the data are at the mercy of the mind of the collector. This happens daily in con-textual interviews with no collection analyst to guide the effort. Whether you are collecting information about customer needs, market trends, or customer satisfaction, throwing it into one big bucket means it is not likely to get used effectively.

Research reservoirs like the Internet and a series of tools for looking at correlations help analysts to fill in the blanks about who, where, and what.

## Vetting Sources

As noted in Chapter 3, spies rarely rely on a single source in their network for a key piece of information. They will play one source against another and approach every bit of intelligence with some skepticism. One important factor if the source of your information is human is motivation: Why did the person give it to you? Does he want something from you in return? Does he stand to gain or lose anything by giving you this information?

In vetting written sources of information as well as spoken, the following are red flags that your source may not be reliable:

• Inconsistency

I went to a web site to do random research on cancer rates in various countries and found one that maintained that China and Japan had lower rates than the United States because of their diet. That may be true for some types of cancer, but their diet doesn't seem to help prevent liver, stomach, and esophageal cancer—all of which show up more in those countries than in the United States.

• Unreasonable amount of consistency

In the aftermath of the British Petroleum oil-well leak into Gulf waters, the National Public Radio program *On the Media* took notice that multiple news sources sounded a lot alike in their reporting. The hosts, Bob Garfield and Brooke Gladstone, got suspicious when, over and over, the comparisons to the *Exxon Valdez* spill in 1989 were identical:

"FEMALE CORRESPONDENT: Twenty years ago, the *Exxon Valdez* spilled 11 million gallons in the water there, and fishermen say they're still healing that . . .

MALE CORRESPONDENT: To put that in per-
spective for you, the *Exxon Valdez* spill dumped 11 million
gallons of oil . . .
MALE CORRESPONDENT: It was tremendous
destructive catastrophe for Alaska, and it was only 11 million gallons of oil."

So *On the Media* invited author and *Exxon Valdez* expert Riki
Ott to explain how that supposed fact crept into all of the news
reports. Ott is a reliable source because she has been vetted by
some very tough critics since the 2008 publication of her book
*Not One Drop: Betrayal and Courage in the Wake of the Exxon Valdez
Oil Spill*. In brief, when media clamored for a verifiable number to
assign to the number of gallons spilled, the Exxon spokesperson
said there might be alcohol involved in the accident. Ott credibly
maintains that at the moment, the if-it-bleeds-it-leads approach to
journalism drove everyone off-topic and riveted their attention
to the issue of alcohol. Thereafter, the number used in stories
remained as 11 million gallons, even though the reality seems to
be closer to 38 million gallons. Sound familiar? Confuse your
source, and he will forget where he was.

• Hyperbole

Some studies suggest that garlic is good for you. Where you go
after that benign and defensible statement can be a far-flung empire
of health benefits that includes melting fat, reducing inflammation,
lowering cholesterol, curing ringworm, preventing blood clots
and cancer, reducing fever and headache, and countering high
blood pressure. Depending on the web site you visit, you might
also find that it cures asthma and arthritis and acts as a deterrent to
invasions from Mars or at least vampires.

• Complexity

There is no reason why anyone communicating with nonex-
perts needs to use four-dollar words to do it. To me, that conveys
the idea that they don't want to be asked questions; I wonder,
"Why not? What are you hiding?"

## Calculating Proximate Reality

In many situations, you must make decisions on the basis of incomplete information. A common deficit would be uncertainty about your competitor's plans, no matter how well you know your competitor. When Saddam Hussein stood ready with his weapons and troops on the fringes of Kuwait, it looked like he would invade, but we didn't know for sure. Even those closest to Saddam could not read his mind.

Lacking certain facts, analysts in the intelligence community create a complete picture by connecting the dots. Arriving at what they call *proximate reality*—an estimate as close to the facts as they can get—reflects the use of logic and creative thinking. Both are necessary, so you come up with answers that make sense, but you also ask "what if?" along the way.

Let's say you want to determine the release date for your main competitor's next product. The facts you have are:

- The competitor has released its new product at the main industry trade show for the past two years.
- The main industry trade show was in late October both of those years.
- The show is in mid-September this year.
- The competitor has a new CEO.
- The competitor has gained market share over the past year, largely due to the success of the last product release.

Logic may tell you that a September introduction is unlikely because of product development cycles, but you don't know if the competitor began that product development cycle early. Industry shows are scheduled years in advance; they were aware of change, just as you were.

Creative thinking helps you get into the mind of the CEO and evaluate statements about why she was hired. Is she aggressive about product development and a first-to-market devotee, or someone who likes to broadside the competition by coming in afterward with a superior or flashier product? Think about her past accomplishments; they are most likely a matter of public record. Is she an organizer who has ramrodded her way to the top of her game?

**Exercise**

Create alternative scenarios by connecting the dots.

Team up with one or more colleagues, with at least one of you being a decided contrarian. Lay out a challenge your department or your company faces; make sure it involves critical missing puzzle pieces. Express the challenge in a simple question such as, "What will their high-profile product offering be next holiday season?" Then:

• Agree on five key facts available to you and use them as a springboard for research.
• After taking whatever time you decide the exercise deserves, reconvene and present your answers.
• Do negative brainstorming to figure out why each one can't possibly be the answer.
• Determine which answer withstood the assault the best. That's your proximate reality.

## Matching Audience and Packaging

There are two types of guidelines here, one of which I'll call background guidelines, and the other, format guidelines.

### Background Guidelines
**You need the answers to these questions related to audience:**
• Who is the main recipient of the research?
• What family of information (financial, product, personnel, timeline, etc.) does that person or group consider most important?
• Is the primary audience an artifact thinker or an icon thinker? Or if your primary audience is a combination of people, such as a board of directors, who is the most influential member of that audience?

The background guidelines are relatively self-explanatory, with the exception of the last question.

Maryann spent many years as a consultant to standards organizations such as technology consortia and groups following the rigorous procedures to create American National Standards for hardware and software. In that time, she presented a number of reports on internal and external communications programs. In general, most audience members were what I referred to in Chapter 1 as "centered artifact thinkers"; that is, they see the task at hand, cut it into component parts, and drive it to completion with confidence they are at the center. It's safe to say that Maryann is a big-chunk iconic thinker, however, so she had to learn (in some cases, the hard way) that her reports on the grand scheme of public relations (PR) activities and their interconnectedness with reputation and long-term goals sent people running to the snack table. They wanted to know what the correlation was between a press release on June 7 and media coverage of the organization. They also wanted to know the correlation between media coverage during the month of June and membership dues.

Here's the ironic conclusion that any readers in public relations will appreciate: She found that an iconic thinker, which describes most effective PR people, may get more headaches than it's worth trying to do PR for a group of artifact thinkers. However, if you want to hang on to your job, deliver the intelligence in a way that makes sense to them.

**Format Guidelines** Your categories of concern here are:
- Data families—What are the discrete categories of information in the research?
- Framework—How do the different types of data fit into the big picture?
- Style—Does the presentation have the language appropriate for the audience?
- Energy—Does the content address the energetic bent of the audience, positive or negative?
- Look and feel—Does the presentation hit the mark for the person, whether impatient or enduring?

**Data Families** Here is a Q&A to illustrate the importance of establishing the family of information in your research. "Data families" simply refers to the correlations people will make with data. Do you need to call out exactly what you mean, or are you okay with simply labeling a box of items "X." If the group is diverse, you will need to clearly illustrate what you mean by each bullet. If the group is insular and shares common language, you are free to write what is considered universal jargon for the category. This is highly dependent on two factors: disposition and exposure.

Question 1:  What is an arrangement of ropes and pulleys?
Question 2:  What are basic football skills?
Question 3:  What are business terms to describe fundamental skills?
    Answer: Block and tackle

Your challenge in business communication will be more complex, of course. You may think that the data you provide on personnel issues are numbers pinned to morale or hiring practices. Your audience may think it belongs in the family of information called "financials" because your intelligence suggests that 20 percent of your workforce is disengaged and should be terminated.

**Framework**   Returning to the earlier example of Maryann communicating with the artifact thinkers, her framework was different from theirs. She had a great, big Christmas tree in mind and proceeded to methodically decorate it for them during her presentation. Their framework was a modest-sized tree, and they wanted to see a star on top of it—nothing else mattered. Decide what you are targeting.

**Style**   You opened this book expecting sharp-edged language that told you how to get the job done, whether it was questioning, negotiating, or whatever you had as a priority. If I sounded like Wayne Dyer (as much as I respect him), you would not have thought, "Hey, I got my money's worth!"
    You don't want to fake a style of communication, but you do want to be smart enough to get some help if you know your vocabulary and tone will offend or bore—or simply not connect—with the audience.

**Energy** I said it in Chapter 1 and I'll say it again: Remove the connotations from the words "positive" and "negative" in terms of what both kinds of energy can bring to your operation. Someone with negative energy may well intend to apply force to accomplishing a positive outcome.

With that in mind, you will want to hit pain points first in your report rather than talk about opportunities if your audience is a negative-energy person. Conversely, some people want a front-loading of good news because it gives them strength to deal with the challenges presented later.

**Look and Feel** Earlier in this chapter, I mentioned that intelligence services would periodically supplement the briefing for Ronald Reagan with short videos. Makes sense for someone with a background in movies. In contrast, Jimmy Carter wanted a level of detail in his briefings that exceeded what people in the intelligence community were accustomed to providing. It's consistent with his academic background—Georgia Institute of Technology and the Naval Academy—and his fascination with nuclear-powered submarines.

Do not ignore what your audience thinks is important in terms of look and feel. You may think it's ideal to hand someone an iPad and let her navigate a presentation herself. You do that with a technophobic paper lover and you will likely put your audience in a mild state of fight or flight.

A critical part of packaging in terms of look and feel is how quickly the person wants the information. Are you dealing with a revolutionary or an organizer, who has a persistent sense of "hurry up"? Or is your audience a legislator or transformer, who will be willing to wait a bit as long as you move steadily to the point?

# Filters Affecting Analysis

This is where the dispositions covered in Chapter 1 really come into play. Every single person has filters that have grown layer by layer as organically as your skin.

As an analyst, you absolutely need to know what kind of person *you* are in terms of disposition so that you can move your biases to the side as much as possible. You need to be able to identify the following:

• Beliefs that are well founded, but false

I watched someone at our office press the security code on the door and then hit the lock button. I said, "All you need to do is hit the lock button."

Her response was not uncommon—nor was it uncommonly stupid. Before anyone had told her that all she had to do was hit the lock button, she presumed that the code was necessary. The door locked, so she got her "reward" for following a process. For that seemingly logical reason, she repeats it every time. It's like the duck that plays the piano because of the corn; not playing the piano to make music, but to eat the corn.

The same thing is true for many of us with processes we do. For example, I have worked with companies that adhere to "project management methodology" or "stage-gate methodology." For some of them, following the rules of the process is the way a lot of Christians say The Lord's Prayer: It's repetition for its own sake. Sometimes it has meaning; sometimes it doesn't. But you'd better darn well say it at the right time. If they get it ingrained into a culture, then it was worth the steps; otherwise, it's needless recitation.

• Faith-based agenda

I am not talking about religious beliefs here, although they are certainly a subset of this discussion. Any analyst is a human being first and an analyst second. That means that she may have hot-button issues relating to personal beliefs.

Remember MOVER from Chapter 3? Analysts are not immune to the impulses sparked by money, opportunity, values, ego, and revenge. As an analyst, you're in a position to deliver the unbiased truth, to illuminate the advantages of something you love, or to disparage something you hate.

Depending on your own disposition, you will make a choice related to values and ego.

CHAPTER 7

# Decide Like a SEAL

**Tools**
- Leverage of subroutines
- Contingency thinking
- Value planning
- After action review (AAR)

You will not see the following bulleted list in some secret SEAL handbook. I have simply taken what I know from my own training and from working alongside SEALs and laid out the steps in a way that applies to your business life.

- Decisions are about something of consequence.
- Your decision builds the next action.
- Know how your decisions affect people in addition to yourself.

The tools covered here lay out the mechanics of decision making so that you can follow the above steps.

I often call Navy SEALs world-class athletes with firearms. Navy SEALs have perfected the art of making life-and-death decisions. This chapter is not what a Navy SEAL himself would tell you, but rather, based on my observation from teaching and being around SEALs, Special Forces soldiers, and other special operations types.

After a month of air strikes that launched Operation Desert Storm, Allied forces stood prepared to begin the ground war against the Iraqis who had invaded Kuwait. About 17,000 Marines waited in ships near Kuwait City as a SEAL team went in to action to dupe Iraqis into thinking that an amphibious attack was imminent. They swam 500 yards in to shore at night—right where the Iraqis were—each SEAL carrying explosives. After planting the explosives, they swam back to their boats. When the bombs went off at 1:00 AM, the SEALs kicked into high gear with the noisemakers: automatic weapons and grenades. Between the sounds of weapons and Marines they spotted off the coast, the Iraqis assumed they were being attacked from the sea. But when they moved their troops toward the coast, the SEALs and Marines were gone. The ground war had begun.

To accomplish a diversion that time-sensitive and dangerous, the SEALs on that mission had a process for decision making that turned science into art. The science was their intense preparation and the muscle memory it engendered; the art was the quick and often innovative decision a person can make under intense pressure because that muscle memory exists. By constantly preparing for specific activities and making those unconscious movements reactionary, they remove the need to think about most of the things they do. In effect, they leave processor space or bandwidth to the decisions that are important.

Anyone in ballet or martial arts understands the science-to-art concept. Dancers learn that they must perfect the basic positions and movements of ballet; once they do, they will be free to dance. In martial arts, you practice the kata over and over. You master these patterns of movement to create muscle memory; you are still the brain that decides "I need to attack this guy to my right, high," but your body automatically moves into the right position once you make that decision.

All military folks learn some of this in their basic training, such as how to respond to an ambush, how to advance on an enemy position, and so on. But most of them move on to much more mundane activities. The basics are still there, but they are hidden away, hopefully to be recalled when needed. Many of these support folks have day jobs that are not directly related to combat. They perform some other task for a living, such as processing payroll, gathering intelligence, or cooking. The only time they practice for war is when they "go to the field" or are actually in war. They prepare for combat when the opportunity arises.

The bill payers (for example, infantry) in every branch of the military are not really doing the primary job they are trained for in peacetime. They are in the business of combat, and they train for life-and-death situations even when not actually engaged in combat.

Preparing for combat is the day job of most special operations people. The key difference is between the basic combat training most of us soldiers received and the training the operators receive is the complexity of the skills—and the fact that they turn them into a packaged process. They start with the most rudimentary of skills like hand position in the kata and they practice hand position on their own weapon until it is a natural part of their daily life. They do the same thing with skills like clearing misfires or any one of hundreds of what we will call *microactivities*.

While honing these actions, they are working on things such as physical endurance for the tasks they need to accomplish. They train as a team on hostage rescue and demolition missions, until even the big pieces are routine and their hands, feet, and bodies do exactly what they have practiced. Much like the martial arts weapons expert, they look like one with the tools they use; more important, they look like one as a team.

This is basic blocking and tackling. It's the time-sensitive, high-pressure exercises involving clearing a bunker, ambushes, and night reconnaissance. You get through that, and your mind is freed up to make the important decisions. You don't waste mental energy on deciding why, if, or how; your decision is where and when.

After every operation, no matter how successful, the team does an after action review, or *AAR*. This allows the team members to look at and discuss the elements that worked and the elements that were not so good. This doesn't mean sitting around and being self-congratulatory. It is a constant sharpening of the knife's edge. The compounding effect of artful individual and team skills with AAR creates a machine-like precision in operation.

The process of deciding like a SEAL, therefore, is not a simple decision tree, which reflects straightforward if-then logic. It is the ability to face an unknown without fear and with your brain capable of engaging in creative problem solving because you have moved past "if-then" to five steps beyond "then."

## Value to Business

Most issues you face daily are hand-position issues, not life-and-death issues. Understanding how to remove the minutia from your daily life frees your mind to make high-impact, powerful decisions with the full application of your intellect. Since you still have to accomplish the hand-position things, you need to establish them as routines and polish them to allow your science to become art. If you are part of a team, taking the same process to your team allows you to clear the clutter and expand your bandwidth to make the important decisions. And if these life-and-death operators can learn from AAR, so can you.

Look at any given issue you face in a day and consider it in two ways.

First, what elements of it can you control, and what elements are things over which you have no control? You will not need to waste decisions on the aspects of the issue you have no control over. Your job there is to mitigate their impact through preparation, such as contingency planning. Those elements you do have control over require you to prioritize according to damage and danger.

Second, what kind of issue is it? The issue is either something you have handled before or something you knew you would handle someday. Sure, there is a first time for everything, but you can be prepared for it. The advantage is that you are not only mentally more capable to handle the challenge, but also emotionally capable of handling it.

The first time Maryann fired someone, she was twenty-six years old. The person was the bookkeeper for the small, nonprofit organization she ran, so Maryann sought advice on the firing from an executive with a financial institution; he was one of her mentors. She said to him, "I need to fire the bookkeeper immediately. How do I do this well?" That mentor taught her the blocking and tackling of firing someone who handles money for an organization, that is, a person who could potentially do a lot of damage very quickly if revenge came into play. (The bookkeeper was a perfect example of the enduring personality who was positioned to snap. Instead of being promoted to a position of more authority, she was going to get fired.) In effect, Maryann had the luxury of a mentor to help her through a tough time. If a Navy SEAL were in this same situation, it is "game over." In special operations terms, it would be the equivalent of deciding you need to rescue hostages at a given location and being taught in the chopper along the way how to do it.

Ideally Maryann would have had the discussion with her mentor months earlier and thought of "what if." She could have wargamed the situation over and over in her head to be prepared for the chance she might need to fire someone in a sensitive position. This is the kind of specific preparation for a challenge that makes it possible to decide like a SEAL.

Theater people and military people have a lot in common. Rehearsal allows you to be in the moment and deliver a powerful and intelligent performance. You know your lines, where to move, and who else is on stage. There will always be surprises, but you can move forward without a glitch as long as you're well rehearsed.

The professional benefit is being able to invest all of your energy in a given activity. Whatever it is you do, you have to be in the moment—you have to be "on." Get to the point where you can describe yourself like that, whether you are in sales, accounting, or occupying a C-suite. So many people sit at their desks and drudge through the day.

Relying on subroutines, pinning value to your decisions, and having the confidence to think through emergencies will take you out of the drudgery and put you into the fun part. Your decisions then show you know what you're doing going into the challenge and have the ability to put the full force of your intelligence into the decision. The result is that your timing and capacity for prioritizing improve measurably. You also have more mental space for innovative thinking.

# Tools of Deciding

## *Leverage of Subroutines*

Take a look at your daily job. How much of what you spend your time doing can be classified a microactivity like the SEAL's hand position on his weapon? Are you expending mental energy on that? Are you deciding every day which color pen to use? Is the shirt you are going to wear for the day a major part of your morning? If it is, you are occupying good brain space with useless items. When your head gets too full and you are forced to make a decision, fight or flight is going to kick in as a result of stress; your ability to think will plummet. When that occurs, the only tools you have are going to be the ones you have committed to muscle memory or have trained under high stress. You already know how to commit these processes to memory; trust yourself. You get into the car every morning or leave your house every morning without thinking about every step of the way. Buttoning your shirt is a microactivity. It is part of a subroutine of getting to work.

Like a SEAL's hand position on his firearm, no single activity is good without the others. Try to see your microactivities as building blocks in your subroutines, that is, chunks of coordinated activity that you can cut and paste into parts of your life. One block might be key in many subroutines; alternatively, you might need it for only one specific thing.

Is negotiating with the YOU WILL HELP transformer in your finance department causing you grief? Have you gotten to the point of impasse over a decision and been dragged into details with him more times than you can count? If so, you are likely allowing your nemesis to engage a critical subroutine he has polished to art.

Here are the mechanics of the process: He relies on a core job skill, which is command of detail. As part of that, he has microactivities related to finding fault with data. He turns that to a quick analysis of trends and supports his finding with details. He has used the same skill set repeatedly to take your argument to the mats, choking your argument with details. You feel as though you have very little wiggle room; your decisions go to piecemeal implementation issues. He succeeds in getting you to decide what color ink to use and not the substance on the paper. This tactic can effectively delay a decision, thereby killing an entire project or alternatively, pushing a project to the next stage that reflects his personal agenda. As this scenario suggests, not every subroutine is a single-use tool; look for places that subroutines can multitask.

Get the subroutines of your daily job to the point they are like starting your car. In the beginning, it will take conscious effort. After a while, you will notice you are not thinking about them anymore.

Body position affects memory. If you find you decide better when you are walking, incorporate it into your daily process. Experiment to see if certain times of the day work better for a given process. If so, then execute the process at that time. One way to reinforce that is to schedule certain types of meetings for certain times of the day. Either way, drill these elements into your subroutine.

**Set Trip Wires** Once you have the subroutines designed for specific functions and see how they can apply in multiple situations, how do you put them to use? Just like a SEAL, set trip wires.

A trip wire sets off a device without the need for human intervention. It can allow one person to cover a lot more area. In effect, the trip wire targets and pulls the trigger on the enemy. The only decision you have to make is where to set the trip wire to get the right bad guy.

In business, this means understanding when to engage your subroutines. In time, your natural response will be to engage your subroutine for conflict three steps before the conflict is unmanageable. Or to engage your subroutine for creating diversion, for example, well in advance of the moment when critical eyes will be on you.

When I taught young interrogators, I would have them create questioning pages for specific topics that would be difficult to prepare for on the fly. By having this available when a chemical weapons expert is captured, the young interrogator could ask the questions needed to exploit the source's information. This is all part of cultivating certain subroutines and giving yourself the mental space to do contingency thinking.

## *Contingency Thinking*

I'm borrowing this term from *Business Lessons from the Edge,* which Maryann wrote with speaker/business consultant Jim McCormick. Contingency thinking is a thought process related to decision making. It builds on contingency planning, which is about having the subroutines in place.

You can't stop a random event from occurring, but if you have a grasp of what decisions are required in a given circumstance, as well as what decisions are possible, then you can mitigate the ill effects.

The morning that King Hussein of Jordan was scheduled to visit the Sikorsky plant in Connecticut, a call came from the Federal Aviation Administration. Of the two S-76 helicopters making the trip from Massachusetts with Hussein and his entourage, one had crashed into a mountain. The King was a pilot and didn't like the weather conditions for flying that day, so he had decided to drive to the plant—but he didn't tell the Sikorsky people.

So for a time, all they knew at Sikorsky was that one of their helicopters assigned to the King of Jordan had crashed and there were fatalities.

Decisions had to be made related to diplomatic protocol, media, and internal communication. And there was a host of subset decisions depending on who had died in the fiery crash.

Bob Stangarone, Sikorsky's lead communications executive at the time, had file folders of "what ifs" and he grabbed the ones that applied to the circumstances at hand. He could focus on setting priorities and serving as a stabilizing force in the maelstrom instead of sorting through a thousand options for next steps.

What Bob did is exactly what I used to tell the young interrogators I taught: "Have an accordion file ready to go to war" (or in today's parlance "have a loaded iPad in your pack"). The point is that you can prepare for random events and a host of emergency situations if you take the time to ask yourself "what if?" and then devote time to exploring the answers when you're not in the midst of the crisis.

You could call any good military professionals superstitious because they are creatures of routine. Same thing with athletes in extreme sports; the rituals of preparation and execution are part of how you keep yourself alive. And to a great extent, it's the same thing with people in business, like Bob Stangarone, who are skilled decision makers.

### Exercise

Set priorities in an emergency.

If the person most central to your operation suddenly died, what decisions would immediately have to be made to keep things running smoothly? How do those decisions interrelate, that is, add value to each other?

Absent those specific decisions, what would happen to your operation?

**Prioritize Targets** An especially good lesson to take from operators is to be in the moment when making a decision. When operators are on site, they have no time to think about issues other than the task at hand. They compartmentalize their lives as a result and focus all attention on each decision. Regardless of what is happening back home or who died yesterday, their minds stay on point. When SEALs or other operators are in combat, they have to categorize people as friend or foe and make decisions about not only which target to neutralize, but also which one is first.

It is a key lesson—and one I count the most important of my life. In basic training, I was in a live-fire exercise and at the end of the exercise, multiple "enemies" simulated by pop-up targets faced us. One had a machine gun firing blanks at me and my buddy. I shot every target as it popped up until my drill sergeant hit me across the helmet with a rifle cleaning rod and barked, "Don't be a dumb ass! You can't kill everybody: Kill the guy with the machine gun!"

Some people make a decision just to make a decision. They might as well wear a T-shirt with the message, "I'm insecure! I reinforce my sense of self by making decisions about things that don't matter!" I knew the president of a company who did this. He decided what color paper would be used for interoffice memos and time sheets. He decided what magazine subscriptions the office would carry. As a result of his decision-making style, his vice presidents easily grabbed power in the company by making decisions that showed the board of directors how misguided and weak the president was.

Commonly, a person like this earns the polite title of micromanager. I'd call him a mini-manager, in that his reach is so small there are serious limitations on what he can accomplish.

It's important not to confuse "little things" with essential details, however. In his 2010 book, *CEO Priorities,* Neil Giarratana devotes an entire section to the power of commanding the right details for the purpose of making important decisions:

> The smart executive, knowing the details, and thinking about them in a three-dimensional manner (what do they mean for all aspects of this project?) will be able to show her talent and power and ability by citing and being able to discuss—mostly from memory—the salient and substantial details of the project or issue currently under discussion. Numbers, facts, actions, reactions—none of this will bother the smart CEO. Instead, she will show a particular joy in being able to juggle all of the relevant facts and details at will, as well as know that, while doing so, she is exercising power in a particularly effective manner.

In short, focus on details that give your ultimate decision more weight and train yourself out of decisions except the ones that matter. You do that by relying on subroutines.

**Identify Targets**   When operators make decisions about targets they have to take into account what's possible. Although they might want to eliminate all of the bad guys, they often are inhibited by obstacles. Which targets can you do something about, and which ones can't you do anything about? Sometimes, you know the target is out there, but it's out of range.

Remember these lessons on having reliable subroutines that will allow you to make quick decisions:

- Know your field of fire. Which targets are in range, and which are not? It is a valid concern, but one that might happen. Contingency think in preparation, but don't consume vital shoot-now time.
- Don't waste bullets while a guy runs behind a tree. If there's a target that won't come out from behind the tree for eighteen months, then wait eighteen months to take a shot; that is, wait until you have a clean shot. Just remember one of the things you learned as a baby: object permanence. When the guy disappears behind a tree, he isn't really gone.
- Prioritize targets. You can't hit everyone, so hit the guy with the machine gun.

- Know what you can change. You waste your time when you get spun up about something you cannot do anything about. Figure out what you can address. You can't change the weather, so if bad weather means your shooting only tells the enemy where you are, then don't shoot.
- Consider sitting tight. Sometimes, the best strategy is sit tight and let the bad guy get tired. This is the military equivalent of the U.S. president's pocket veto, or the finance department you will help in the earlier story.
- And one final lesson: When I went to Kuwait, one of the very experienced noncommissioned officers (NCOs) said to me, "Mr. Hartley, I want to teach you a valuable lesson: Shoot them in the feet. They wear Kevlar body armor, including face masks, but nobody wears Kevlar shoes." This is a good double-edged lesson for daily life.
  - Look for the easy targets; get them out of the way and then work on the hard ones.
  - Even the tough problems have an easier and a harder solution than the ones you first thought of—if you're innovative.

The minute you have priorities to deal with, treat them like an operator would treat clearing a building: They become your singular focus. Worrying about the impact of a decision after you have already weighed all variables prevents you from being able to make a decision in a timely manner. Most operators use terms such as "bad guys" to talk about targets. It puts the enemy in a box and dehumanizes the target. You have to put the issue in the box and take away its potency, its ability to bite back. Then you can kill it.

**Intersect Fields of Fire**  Any military operation from squad to theater will have overlapping fields of fire. It prevents gaps the enemy can exploit. This means each of the operators in a team backs up his buddies and no one is vulnerable to attack. If you think about your daily operations, are you creating supporting fire for the rest of your team, or are you the stand-alone type? Every decision SEALs make is additive to the next, and each of their actions has an overlapping effect to eliminate outcomes for the enemy and leave options for the team.

## Value Planning

Operators view decisions as building blocks. The decision should build toward further action; it should add value to your next step.

If you were to catalog all the decisions in your organization in a single day, how many would be disconnected from the mission or unsupportive of it? Worse yet, some would most likely be counter-productive. Your personal decisions, and those made throughout your organization, would ideally line up like skydivers in a choreo-graphed jump. In a formation like this one, everyone doesn't show up at once; there is a build of one person on another, with each one making it possible for the next jumper to dock on the forma-tion (see Figure 7.1).

If you considered your decisions in these terms, you could avert, or at least mitigate, pitfalls like tunnel vision on your project management and decisions that serve as roadblocks to the success of other people in your company.

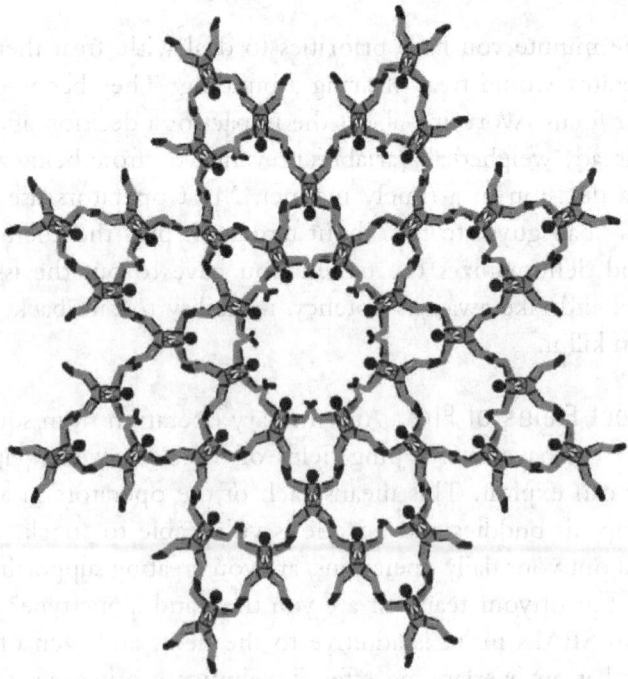

FIGURE 7.1   Each decision adds value to the next.

**Exercise**

Identify a decision of yours that added value and plot the result.

Take a look at Figure 7.1. Consider the inner ring a decision you made that allowed other good decisions to build upon it. Follow it out three or four steps.

**Exercise**

Identify a decision of yours that could not be built on and plot the result.

Here, you are doing the opposite of the preceding exercise. In skydiving, the effect is that you might come into the formation too fast, go lower than someone else, or flail. The effect is that the person who is supposed to dock on you can't do it and the formation fails.

## *After Action Review (AAR)*

If your organization does not conduct AARs, why not? Are you better prepared and more machine-like than a SEAL team?

Even successful client meetings and interteam meetings can benefit from a simple AAR. You set up a safe environment to cover what went right, what went wrong, and lessons learned. You can formalize the process or simply have informal meetings. People grow and learn best from epiphany, so asking questions will cause people to create their own ideas and internalize the lesson better. In the end, you sharpen the very skills that made your meeting a success or replace the ones that caused failure.

SEALs experience component-based training. All of their training ingrains subroutines. They link those subroutines together in order to make decisions quickly. In a high-pressure situation, muscle memory forces their finger to go to the right place on the trigger housing. It puts their feet in the right position and gets them to move in a coordinated fashion with their team. All they are doing is linking subroutines together so that their brain can remain focused on making decisions.

If you have to think about every incremental step, you will be a bad decision maker.

You do not have such a tiny memory that you have to sift through redundant details every time you have to make a decision; otherwise, you would have the brain of a rodent. Train yourself to rely on subroutines so that your brainpower is focused on the decisions that matter.

If you've been in a consumer products business for twenty years and you haven't seen 90 percent of the predicaments that occur in that business, you haven't been paying attention. Your business is laced with the same problems over and over. Rely on that knowledge to create a set of microactivities that compound to subroutines. Then create some trip wires to engage those subroutines. You can't engage every target, so prioritize the ones you can and focus all of your energy on the targets you want to neutralize, realizing what is possible and not forgetting the one hiding behind the tree. Work with your allies to create overlapping fire and let them make decisions that support you. And when all the shooting stops, revisit the outcome. You will be surprised how much more bandwidth you have than you think you do.

CHAPTER 8

# Team-Build Like
# Special Ops

**Tools**
- Rite of passage
- Homogenizing
- Top-grading

The way you build teams depends on your mission.

Special Forces units of the U.S. Army have a mission to train and counsel indigenous people so that they can defend their own freedom and establish their own government. Their motto captures that mission: *De Oppresso Liber* (Latin: To Liberate the Oppressed). Their team structure, therefore, allows them to be nimble.

A conventional military organization chart is stovepipes of enlisted personnel leading up to commanders. From battalion to company to platoon, every person hears the same order; it's echoed down. Special Forces has a different arrangement to reflect their mind-set and requirements to fulfill their mission. The Special Forces model is more like a Venn diagram with the team leader/team chief in the center and members of the team overlapping. They are functionally focused.

The team consists of a medic and experts in engineering, weapons, communications, and intelligence. They find out what a guy is good at when he arrives in the team, and then start to cross-fertilize. The whole then becomes worth more than the sum of the parts. And although the team members blend and meld, ultimately developing a common character, the men themselves retain whatever personalities and quirks they brought with them.

The character the team develops is unique to that team and unique to that moment. Teams do not last forever. They occupy a spot in time that can never be recreated.

## Value to Business

Once upon a time, many companies hired like the Army hires enlisted men and women: If you meet certain minimum requirements and promise to be loyal, you can get a job. To say that's rare in business now is a gross understatement. Companies have to have high selection standards and need teams in marketing, human resources (HR), product development, and every other area that can fulfill their missions without a lot of hand-holding.

The team-building formula makes it clear how to populate those teams and strengthen them.

## Formula for Team Building

The formula for team building is simple, but very few companies get it right.

1. Establish a threshold each team member must get past; consider it a rite of passage; earn the right to prove yourself.
2. Create a homogenized group, blending different types to create a new type.
3. Create room for growth.
4. Clearly define expectations and when someone has no capacity for growth to meet them, eliminate that person.
5. As you top-grade, sustain a culture of growth/change to allow new people to integrate.

## Tools of Team Building
### *Rite of Passage: Passing the Threshold*

Special Forces Assessment and Selection (SFAS) is three weeks of absolute hell. When you step into the program, it doesn't matter what rank you are. You get a number. You are candidate 4 assigned to Team Bravo. In that twenty-one-day process, you might be "peered out" at a particular point; that is, the people around you do not want you around them anymore. You might be dropped in day 7 or you might be dropped on day 21. You might be dropped on day 7 and not be told until day 21.

You can be pushed out by your peers, cut by an instructor, or quit. The intent is to force you to quit.

SFAS happens at Fort Bragg, where the SERE school is, and it involves physical challenges complicated by mentally challenging tasks. Here's a typical SFAS challenge: They give your team a vehicle with three wheels and you have to move it five miles. It might be fun except that you're on a timeline and you haven't slept or eaten in three days. If you don't quit, the exercise illustrates how well you perform despite having lost your edge.

The SFAS web site (www.training.sfahq.com/assessment_ and_selection_sfas.htm) specifies that the program assesses tactical skills, leadership, physical fitness, motivation, and ability to cope with stress. Regarding the latter, the web site says:

**When you report to Fort Bragg, North Carolina**
You should be at 100 percent physical ability with zero percent stress level.

Any of the following might cause you stress while attending SFAS:

Wife not in agreement with you.

Financial problems at home.

Medical problems with yourself or family.

Not sure SF is what you want.

Low self-esteem or lack of motivation.

Not in top physical shape for SFAS.

Just to escape your present unit or duty assignment.

SFAS is just the beginning, but it is one hell of a beginning. It separates those who want to be there from the pretenders. The people who come out the other side still have a lot of proving to do, but they have earned the right to prove themselves.

What is the threshold for belonging on most company teams? Commonly, it's getting hired. That's not good enough. The more formal, the better—and I don't mean something in writing from the HR department.

A rite of passage can be simple or complex, but it is something you can define and describe.

Most likely, you belong to some kind of team at work, regardless of whether you call it a team or a department or a committee. What is the threshold over which everyone must pass to be part of your team?

---

### Exercise

Establish a rite of passage.

You are asked to lead a yearlong project.

1. Based on the categories of action styles described in Chapter 1, put together a team of five people for this intense, twelve-month effort.
2. What would be an appropriate and effective rite of passage for your new team?

As you can see, there is no stock answer in an exercise like this. The rite of passage would have to reflect what kind of bonding mechanism would hit home with the types of people you choose. For example, since the project is a yearlong project, you might be inclined to pick legislators, because they use positive energy to work though a known system, enduring to a desired outcome. But then who will light a fire under the group? Who would question incremental progress to see if it really is progress?

The way people become part of the team may be by making a presentation about how they can help make the project a success or bringing certain resources to the table. The point is that everyone has to do it, and when it's over, team members know something about each other that engenders respect and trust.

---

## The Homogenizing Process

After SFAS, you still have a couple of years of training to complete. They weed people out all along the way. At the very end, the challenge is SERE school, God willing, the worst experience of their lives.

A lot of people quit SF training because it isn't just physically brutal, it's psychologically and emotionally brutal. What I know about this is that they wear your body down to the point where all you have left is your psyche. You have no energy. You might not even have skin on the bottoms of your feet. You have to rely on a sense of purpose, the energy charge you get from your teammates, and your belief in self. Throughout the training, it is each man against himself, and the only way you get through that well is by learning to collaborate with other people.

Along the way, this Special Forces training starts to create common ground and common language. They turn this group of individuals who struggled through the rite of passage known as SFAS into a band of brothers known as Special Forces. These people have core skills in common and other skills that are complementary. They speak, hear, walk, and think alike. The result is a bond few can ever get. Although they might come from various backgrounds in the beginning, they are distilled to team players.

### Lesser Bonds; Creating Blended Teams   When I was working
at SERE school, we were always commanded by a Special Forces officer. SF soldiers normally do not work side by side with non–SF soldiers, so John F. Kennedy Special Warfare Center and School (SWIC), which houses SERE, is an unusual situation. Duty at SERE school is consistent with what Special Forces soldiers do anyway. They are teachers by nature and training; it's their job to go into a country and train people so that they can stand up for themselves.

In addition to Special Forces and interrogators, SERE school also brings in the talents of Delta Force operators and Rangers. You have the need to form teams out of people who are wired differently and groomed differently.

Even with these groups, in order to mesh, there are rites of passages. Most important, to gain credibility with the other instructors, you had to have completed the course yourself. All instructors went through the course eventually, but if you were an instructor who hadn't completed it yet, your acceptance was limited. You could have an opinion about how someone performed, but you couldn't have an opinion about why he did what he did.

You had to pass over the threshold.

After you did, people might make jokes about how you behaved at some part of the course, but nothing was mean spirited. Ever. Your mistakes were obvious, but so were everyone else's. No one goes through SERE school without making mistakes.

Sometimes we would have "rental interrogators" come in to supplement the instructor pool. (We called them renegators.) They hadn't been through the school, so they might make comments that really cut. Just imagine what we did to them. They were never part of the team—no matter how long they stayed.

Going through the rite of passage allowed you to have an opinion. You could now join the team and had earned the opportunity to prove yourself as part of the team. No status other than "peer" is granted by rites of passage, but what better status is there? Also realize that being a peer on the SERE side did not necessarily make the other interrogators, Special Forces, or commanders see me as their peer in rank, expertise, or abilities. It allowed me a one-facet peerage. So I call that a "lesser bond." It also allowed me to do anything at the compound instead of simply interrogate. I was on the road to personal growth.

I still needed to learn all of the tasks to bring my skill set to parts of the job other than interrogation and to learn the ways, skills, and language of my new tribe. In the next few years, that is exactly what happened; then I became part of a very exclusive group called SERE instructors. Our ranks consisted of a motley crew of Special Forces, Intel, retirees, and even an occasional support guy. In our unique way, through specialized language, uniforms, and behaviors, we were homogenized.

You might not have the same opportunity to put your people through two years of hell to learn to be better teammates, but you can take a lesson from these sessions. After you create the rite of passage, you will have an insular space. Then you can create a bonded team in much the same way these special operations people are bonded by using rituals of belonging. These rituals include:

1. Language
2. Timing
3. Shared responsibility
4. Strength for weakness

5. Hardship
6. Reward

**Language** Language is the human's unique tool. Maryann and I have a ritual when writing. We talk. She puts things on paper and sends it to me. I tweak the content, and then she modifies it and sends it back to me. Sometimes I write in English, usually early in the process. But as we get to a more feverish pitch, I simply slam my ideas on to paper. The results are more akin to Greglish than English. It means that Maryann more than nearly anyone else has learned to interpret this pattern of written language; we have our own code. No one else is privy to it, so we have a bond there. You can do this with spoken language too. Create a jargon specific to the team as a bonding mechanism; build "secret knowledge" into your communication so the team has information and ideas that are unique to them. Special Forces members have plenty of these—enough to create a dictionary. Common language and shared secret knowledge create insulation and skepticism regarding outsiders.

**Timing** Creating rituals around cadence of what is and is not allowed behind closed doors means the outsiders cannot fit. It recreates a point of difference. Timing creates insulation and dependence on the trust of others in the group.

**Shared Responsibility** When you go through hell with someone, you often think of that person as a friend. There are tons of adages about this, such as "the devil you know versus the devil you don't." Fundamentally, this is related to needing someone you can trust and having faith in that person to move you to the positive side of the *y*-axis in the action matrix. By creating a reason for people to trust one another, that is, by establishing interrelated objectives that demonstrate trust in the others, you create a more cohesive team. Lame exercises like falling back into one another's arms do not accomplish this. Few people, no matter how morally corrupt, are going to let you fall on the concrete, particularly if someone else is looking. Real trust is built through a person giving of himself for you.

**Strength for Weakness** Give the team a task that forces each person to contribute, but don't tie it to the individual contributions. Stage it so that they are compelled to find the hidden talents of their teammates. Put them in situations that cause them to rely on one another. And use tools to help them make decisions about who brings what to the table if they can't sort through the options.

I was in a reserve Special Forces unit immediately after the Gulf War, not as an interrogator but as a nonqualified SF medic. That means I was earning my right to go to SFAS. (I never did before the unit moved to the National Guard in another state.) The program I was in was about gaining points on an order-of-merit list and waiting for an opening in SFAS. It consisted mostly of brutal physical endeavor, from running to marching with a rucksack to 600-meter swims in uniform with a ruck.

One of the tests involved two-person teams swimming across Victory Pond at Ft. Benning with rucks, followed by running a certain distance to a truck. I had a teammate named McAlister who couldn't swim well. But we had to swim. He was bigger and stronger than I was on land, so I would pull him through the water, wear myself out, and then count on him to drag me through the woods for a while. The team-building effect is to create trust between the two and move both of us up the $y$-axis.

**Hardship** You can create hardship like the "enemy" SERE commander to pull your people together or orchestrate challenging timelines and projects that cause you all to suffer together to create trust. One of the closest bonds I've had in the air-conditioning business was when I first started and shared a very small office with another HVAC construction project manager. During the summer, we were on ridiculous schedules that caused insane stress. We sat five feet apart. When we knew there would be shouting on phone calls, we took turns making calls. I was as close to him as the two psychological operations guys I drove around with in Kuwait during Desert Storm. Hardship can be a powerful catalyst for insulation and trust.

**Reward** By sharing reward, people get a sense of a job well done and reliance on one another. A shared reward can cement trust and strengthen team spirit. I often shared bonuses when I worked in the construction industry for that very reason. We were rowing for the same goal.

I ran an operations team for Trane for three years and brought people across the threshold with a specific way of communicating and a standard of treatment. We were like a family, even though we had only ever met face to face one time. Our virtual team was scattered throughout the country. Despite the distance, everyone looked out for each other.

Why?

- We felt insular. We developed a common vocabulary, had a cadence to our meetings, and certain rituals that streamlined how we communicated. One of the phrases people used was in reference to calling me in to take care of a problem. When the need arose, the person would say, "I need your boot on this guy's neck today." These weren't a bunch of military guys talking like that; almost everyone on the team was female.
- We operated like a real family. In a normal family, not the *Brady Bunch*, you can vent and let other people in your family know how you feel. You create a space where it's okay for people to resolve their problems. You can't create artificial harmony that surfaces for thirty minutes once a week. It has to be real and enduring, and it has to reflect a desire to resolve issues.
- We had secret knowledge; that is, we shared information and ideas only with the team. Things like sharing this book can create a feeling of distinct belonging much like the Freemasons create.

**Room for Growth** You need your own version of the Special Forces Venn diagram to cultivate the kind of growth that reflects joint commitment to the mission. For example, on a sales team everyone can sell. After that, it's a matter of one person being great at reporting, another having amazing research skills, and someone else showing a talent for rapport building. There is no reason why everyone can't get reasonably good at reporting, research, and rapport building. That takes training and practice. You will still have those three people excelling in their respective skill areas, but they will have strong backup.

You need to allow some of it to happen naturally and find areas to develop others if they don't step up. Let people know what weaknesses they need to enhance and how to polish their strengths.

The process of advancing and the ongoing dynamic must have constant reinforcement so that anyone new coming in will know how things work and what's expected of her. If the process is too rigid and the relationships calcified, then anyone new to the team will feel like an outsider. Keep it fluid so the organism can continue to evolve.

One of the worst things the Army ever instituted was "up or out." Before that, you could spend your career being a private and being the best private in the country. For some people, that was true opportunity. The up-or-out program does away with a lot of people who would be excellent, reliable privates; think Radar in *M\*A\*S\*H*.

You need to think about what your people do well. Make sure they understand what they do is a profession. Reward them for doing it well. Do not go out of your way to promote them unless they strive for promotion.

## Top-Grading

"You can't carry the weight" is a literal fact when you're talking to a fellow member of a Special Forces team who's hurt his back. The same honest message must sometimes be delivered to a member of your team who does not have the ability to do the job required. Being direct like that is not essentially mean, but some people lack the rapport-building skills to make the statement without wounding the person.

In conveying that kind of message, you have to make it about the job and not the person. Whatever you can do to help the individual transition to a suitable slot, do it.

A young woman who was tiny—less than 100 pounds—was assigned to my unit in Korea. We were friends; I liked and respected her. One afternoon we were in MOPP (Mission Oriented Protective Posture) gear. Ours was quilted, chemical protective gear, a charcoal filter for your entire body—that included rubber boots, a rubber mask, and rubber gloves. And it was 100 degrees. At the time, I was serving as the assistant to the Nuclear, Biological, Chemical (NBC) officer.

The tiny woman put her mask on but didn't have enough breath to push the filters open. That caused her to take in her own breath over and over, hyperventilate, and go into a seizure. She was suffocating to death. We pulled her mask off.

The commander barked, "What's up?"

"Sir, you need to put her out of the Army," I said.

"What?"

"You can't have this in the Army. She's dead weight."

He agreed with me. She could not meet minimum standards, so her presence contributed nothing to our operations. In fact, she jeopardized them.

She could be reassigned to dead-end office work for a while, but ultimately there was no way to fix the fact that she could not meet the basic physical requirements of a soldier.

If you drag someone like that with you because you don't want her to be left behind, you are being selfish with respect to the team. Once you alert someone to the fact that they cannot perform, if that person does not act honorably and quit, then you have to initiate the termination. Sometimes, it's not even a matter of honor or ego but of simple self-awareness. My friend's son played soccer for one season when he was a kid. He's twenty now and told me recently, "I stunk." But at the end of the season, they gave him a little trophy. He was offended. This is a young man with genuine self-esteem and he knew that trophy meant nothing. Think about all the other kids who also stunk and also got trophies. How many of them came to a realization that they deserved something just for showing up?

Their attitude is the workplace equivalent of "I deserve this job because I'm breathing."

It's okay to state minimum qualifications and objectives and to follow that up by cutting loose anyone who doesn't meet them. Just be honest, "If you're under four feet tall, you cannot ride this ride."

There is a kind and professional way to handle that process, of course.

A Special Forces commander will rarely chew someone out in public. No one will know what happened. If the individual is unfit for the unit, he will be removed—that's how everyone will know. When someone "disappears," therefore, people are sometimes surprised.

Typically, commanders will try to build on your strengths and move you ahead. They are not loud about what you've done wrong; they are smart about getting you to do things right.

In the business world, you might have a team of nine people. Everyone knows who's pulling her weight and who is not. If you tear into the one who is not, you destroy morale. The best way to handle a nonperformer is to counsel her quietly and then get rid of her when she doesn't come through.

Set a timeline. If you privately counsel that nonperformer and then wait and wait to gauge improvement, other people on the team will think you are showing favoritism. You need to set a deadline with her: "This month, you are a 3 on a scale of 1 to 10. If you aren't at least a 5 by next month, I will ask you to find another position." Trust me; if you don't do something eventually, she will get peered out and then your skills will be in question.

## Mechanics of Team Leadership

- Understand your role.
- Keep everyone's head pointed in the same direction so that they can accomplish the mission.
- Remain authentic—deference is a double-edged sword.
- Deal with differences.

### Understand the Role

"Manage" is a synonym for "control." "Lead" is a synonym for "direct." Think of that in any discussion about the difference between managing and leading. Richard Cartwright, a retired Special Forces soldier, was one of my mentors in SERE school. He used to rail about the Army creating managers, not leaders. People could get very good at either ordering, "I say, you do," or responding without question to those orders. That is not the Special Forces way.

You may be a solid leader and not inspire anybody, so do not confuse leadership with motivational speaking any more than you confuse it with management.

Leadership requires the ability to build a team that allows them to shine. Your glory comes from their success. The leader's role is to facilitate what people on his team do well.

A good team leader takes out obstacles in your way. It's not about telling you how to do something, but rather setting objectives, handing over the reins, and asking you what you need to do your job. That's how an effective Special Forces team leader operates.

If that person began as the team medic and then got promoted to a leadership role, he will not stop being qualified as a medic but he will have to drop the role of medic. If he doesn't, he will destroy the confidence of the team medic and stifle his ability to grow. The best learning comes through epiphany. The great team leader asks him questions using the five-question methodology to help the junior medic come to the right conclusion. If he can't get it, because the senior person has acumen and experience that might help him, he needs to step in and privately counsel him.

Similarly, the sales professional who becomes team leader has to abandon the role of selling and embrace the role of mentor. If she doesn't, she will smother her own baby.

Someone in a leadership role can also do something just as deadly by moving too far in the opposite direction. The person who clears obstacles for his team and obstinately protects them "no matter what" will lose sight of their shortcomings and lose sight of the mission.

"Mission first and people always" should be your motto. If your mission is not accomplished, it will result in the destruction of your people.

## *Keep the Team Unified*

Once you have the team bonded, watch their baselines. Stay alert for any signs of fracturing and, as soon as you notice that, use the tools that strengthen interpersonal bonds. If necessary, you could be like the Special Forces commander. He orchestrated situations in which we would naturally bond against him—not in a long-term way, but in a way that brought us closer for the duration of a particular challenge. We didn't hate him; we respected him. But instead of seeing tasks as personal responsibility or isolating emotionally from other people on the team, his actions engendered a sense of shared responsibility and perspective. This is a dangerous, but effective, technique.

## *Do Not Fall Victim to Deference*

Deference is a double-edged sword. At some point, when people defer to you, if you rest on what people defer to you about, you stop growing; you stop gaining. This will strain, if not destroy, the credibility of a leader faster than it will a junior member of a team whom everyone presumes has a long way to go to know "everything."

You may have spent your career in contract law, and others assume you know the a-to-z information about it. Because they assume you do, you never say that you don't. Your ignorance about "f" and "t" may persist for a lifetime because you have never been asked about them specifically, or when you were, you hedged and got away with it. You never raised your hand in class and said, "I don't understand that."

Now that you head the legal department of a huge publishing conglomerate, are you going to raise your hand? It's human nature that someone who has earned deferential behavior from others would not want to blow his cover.

If you are the person being deferred to, admit what you don't know and find the answers. The alternative is that your leadership will have the taint of a lie. Have people close to you who will help you honestly evaluate your performance at meetings and the substance of your written communication.

If you are dealing with a person who has traditionally been deferred to on a regular basis—perhaps that person is your leader or the person considered the smartest person on your team—and you want to build a relationship with her, you need to be sure you pick the audiences very carefully where she might be exposed for what she doesn't know.

You may want to set her up to show what she doesn't know in front of people who "don't matter"; in this way, she gets the message that she needs to overcome her deficit without losing face. Or you may want to set her up to show what she doesn't know in front of people who can break her career and then rescue her before that happens.

Inadvertently, Maryann once faced the latter situation. She had arranged a series of media briefings for the new boss shortly after he took over as president of the company. She trusted the organization's board of directors to have chosen someone who knew at least the basics of the various laws and agreements that profoundly affected their industry. She was only partially right. At the first meeting, the reporter asked for the new president's opinion on a major trade agreement. The new boss turned to Maryann, begging her with his eyes to bail him out. She jumped in with, "I should first say that, historically, the organization considers the agreement to be . . . ."

Her new boss was so grateful to her for giving him context and background—and enabling him to move smoothly to an answer—that a bond immediately developed between them. He knew he could trust her to watch out for him.

Another way to go is to determine what the individual doesn't know and then publicly say, "Why don't you come and teach this at our off-site meeting on Friday?" By taking that approach, you create pressure on him to fill the hole in his knowledge that may be jeopardizing your operation.

It's possible to do this unintentionally, too. If you don't know what he doesn't know and say, "Why don't you come and teach this?" you might see him implode.

## *Deal with Differences*

I mentioned earlier in the chapter that those of us teaching at SWIC were part of the last training challenges that Special Forces candidates faced before earning their full status in Special Forces. One of those tests is called Robin Sage, in which they have to operate with native people as they would on a real mission.

Trainers create an artificial culture for this exercise. At the time my buddies at SWIC conducted the exercise, everyone training the Special Forces candidates spoke Arabic, so they simply used their Arabic throughout the exercise. The Special Forces guys didn't know the language, just as they most likely wouldn't when sent to a real foreign culture.

Part of Robin Sage is that you're encouraged to build a religion and all other elements of a society. In the particular test that my fellow instructors conducted, they built the customs and norms on what they knew. For example, a few times a day, everyone had to pray. But to what? Keep in mind this is a culture created solely as an exercise. On the way to the site, somebody found a big plastic bird—and in extreme opposite of Arab culture, several times a day, everyone in the exercise prayed to Big Bird.

My friend Paco, who was the "religious leader," would read from the Holy Book five times a day. The Holy Book was a copy of *Forum* magazine. Let me quote Wikipedia in describing it: "*Penthouse Forum*, sometimes simply *Forum*, is a magazine owned by the publishers of *Penthouse* magazine. Unlike the main *Penthouse* title, *Penthouse Forum* is more journalistic than pornographic, and features editorials and opinion pieces on controversial contemporary topics."

The Special Forces people had a duty to comply and think through all of the convoluted stuff because a foreign culture will always have some aspects that seem ridiculous. As soldiers in the Special Forces, they would have to exhibit cooperation and leadership with people who didn't think the way they did, behave the way they behaved, or express themselves in a way that seemed familiar.

Even if you've handpicked your team and everyone seems to speak the same language, nobody thinks that same way you do. You may follow the same process and have the same physiological components, but you and the next guy are different. And some of what he does will seem ridiculous to you.

You want to be able to be part of and to lead teams of complementary personality types and action styles, so there are many times when you won't exactly speak the same language—even if you use the same words.

If you're going to deal with the differences, you need to be aware of what they are. And then you decide whether each difference is a source of strength for the team, has a neutral effect, or is tearing the operation apart. Use the matrices on disposition and action styles to help you sort that out and then take action accordingly.

CONCLUSION

# Backbone or No Backbone

When I left the Army, I could not predict how important some of these interpersonal skills would become. I prefer a very open and confrontational style, but I can shift gears if need be. Fortunately, right after leaving the Army, I began working for a very good company that espoused openness.

This book explains tools of the intelligent and special operations world. Make no mistake: Many of them are conniving and underhanded. Even in a company that mandates openness, there are pockets of covert behavior, and these tools are useful when dealing with the people associated with it. Others are simply internal tools to help you think differently; still others arm you with ways to make someone back down. If you are overly polite or politically correct, the confrontational ones will pose challenges for you.

Male and female minds will find different tools easier to use due to subtlety of communication styles. This is just a matter of the way our brains are wired.

Using many of the tools in this book requires behavior that may be strange to you, whether you are a man or a woman. The behavior that may arouse discomfort is deliberate, calculated interaction with other people in order to get specific outcomes. Let's look at the reasons why that behavior is strange as a way of understanding how to go about changing the status quo.

Open aggression of the style used by dogs is characteristically male. Snarling, baring teeth, and backing down opponents with shows of force have worked in micro- and macrosituations for millennia. Traditionally, open confrontation of this sort existed in all walks of American life from the military to the floors of Congress.

Subtle aggression is characteristically female. With the nuances of language and communication, women have gotten their point across without overt shows of force. Is it "unenlightened" to face tough situations head on and express honest judgments and opinions? A lot of people seem to think so, and as a result, we have an increasingly feminized society.

Political correctness is the result of feminine influence. A rugged opinion will offend someone; women tend to avoid offering a deliberately offensive statement.

The controversy over President Barack Obama's choice of a successor for General David H. Petraeus puts a spotlight on this issue. His choice is a tough Marine named James N. Mattis. In 2005—five years ago as of this writing—General Mattis made some pointed remarks at a forum in San Diego: "You go into Afghanistan, you got guys who slap around women for five years because they didn't wear a veil. You know guys like that ain't got no manhood left anyway, so it's a hell of a lot of fun to shoot them."

I've stood shoulder-to-shoulder with Marines; I respect General Mattis for his honesty and the fact that he has a clear picture in his head of who the bad guys are. As for whether or not he's right for a role requiring more diplomacy than he cares to offer, I say, "Do not ask a Marine to act like a social worker. Appoint a social worker."

When men who have a natural tendency to do in-your-face communication grasp that it is unacceptable in the work environment, they turn passive-aggressive. The result can be bizarre and make people truly uncomfortable. Others realize a conflict exists, but it's never obvious. That makes it hard to resolve. It is the elephant in the room that everyone ignores.

In the movie *Yellowbeard*, Harvey "Blind" Pew (John Cleese) has unmatched expertise with a sword, even though he's blind. In a plot to kill him, his enemies put headstones in front of him as he's walking; as he taps the stones he thinks he's at a wall and turns. By doing that, they lure him into a shed full of explosives.

That's how passive-aggressive behavior works.

With more women in control in the workplace, men are playing in an arena they are not equipped for. In attempts to communicate more like women, they are becoming passive-aggressive.

Step back and look at the chasm between a direct, respectful approach to interacting with others and a politically correct one. At its inception, political correctness was intended to show respect for people who are "different" in some way and to bring us together. Now, instead of broadcasting openness to others and genuine respect for them, it's become a methodology for pandering. It is a subjugating influence.

Men and women bring different capabilities and skill sets to communications that reflect the different designs of our brains. Use both in your business to get to the right answers. Stop pretending we are the same. "Equal" is not synonymous with "identical."

Men and women need to work together in the workplace to return political correctness to its original role and move discussions into the territory of honest, straightforward communication.

That takes backbone. I want to share one of my primary rules of business—and of life—as a way of helping you strengthen your backbone: Never defer to stupidity.

It's critical that you communicate concerns within the bounds of appropriate language and behavior, but you must be clear and direct. You observe a breach of ethics or a financial lapse, for example, and you must open your mouth. You have the right to do that no matter what your role is.

No one will hate you if you grow a backbone. If they do, don't worry about it. They will come to respect you later.

"You have enemies? Good. That means you've stood up for something, sometime in your life."

—*Winston Churchill*

# GLOSSARY

**AAR:**  an abbreviation for after action review; the team review of an operation to pinpoint what went right and what went wrong, and why.

**Action matrix:**  a foundation tool of profiling developed by Gregory Hartley to predict how, and how soon, a person will act.

**Active listening:**  using body language to show interest in what a person is saying.

**Adaptors:**  movements to release nervous energy.

**Agent:**  person who provides intelligence.

**Anchor point:**  an idea that makes a source feel attached to the subject at hand, for example, a statistic about product $x$ failure rates given to a customer thinking of buying product $x$.

**Approaches:**  psychological ploys to extract information.

**Artifact thinker:**  sees discrete packages of information in every concept or conversation (also see "icon thinker"); a term coined by Gregory Hartley.

**Asset:**  someone who facilitates covert operations; may be the bridge between the case officer and the agent.

**Barriers:**  movements and tools that help you protect your space.

**Baseline:**  the way a person behaves and speaks normally.

**Behavioral Interview Technique Enhanced (BITE):**  a four-step process for job interviewing that involves asking non-traditional questions, looking for leads, prioritizing leads, asking follow-up questions, and repeating the process; developed by Gregory Hartley.

**Canned question:**  a question rooted in research you did on a topic you knew you would be discussing with someone knowledgeable about that topic.

**Compound question:** a question with more than one answer, for example, "Did you take the highway and then go to the office or take the back road and end up at the office after lunch?"

**Contingency thinking:** a term coined by Maryann Karinch and Jim McCormick to describe a thought process for decision making that builds on contingency planning.

**Control question:** a question to which you know the answer; very useful in establishing a person's baseline.

**Direct question:** a straightforward question, for example, "What are you doing here?"

**Disposition matrix:** a foundation tool of profiling developed by Gregory Hartley to describe the relationships of altruism versus selfishness and collectivism versus individualism and how those relationships are affected by compassion.

**Elicitation technique:** method of getting a source to talk to you in a focused way without divulging your true intent.

**Extreme Interpersonal Skills:** a term coined by Gregory Hartley to describe the suite of human behavior skills that arm you with the ability to read and manipulate people.

**False-flag recruitment:** someone pretends to represent the cause you espouse, but in fact, is recruiting for the other side.

**Fight or flight:** a state of stress in which the body prepares itself automatically to either take on a threat or run away from it.

**Five-questions technique:** a quick way of using common interests to shift a conversation to a topic about which you are knowledgeable; common to intelligence collection and part of the extreme interpersonal skills suite.

**Follow-up question:** one that is hooked onto a response to the previous question.

**Fulfillment Strategy, The:** a term coined by Gregory Hartley to describe a three-step process of giving someone an incentive to become an active part of your network.

**HUMINT:** an abbreviation for human intelligence; refers to the source of the information.

**Icon thinker:** sees correlations between pieces of information (also see "artifact thinker"); a term coined by Gregory Hartley.

**Illustrators:** movements that punctuate your statements.

**IMINT:** an abbreviation for image intelligence; refers to the source of the information.

**Leading question:** one in which the questioner projects an answer.

**Legislator:** uses positive energy to work though a known system enduring to a desired outcome.

**Microactivities:** components of more complex activities that can be mastered so that doing them does not require thought every time.

**Microinterview:** a questioning technique in which you dig progressively deeper into the specifics of a story.

**Minimizing:** making the consequences of the issue seem less than they really are.

**MOVER:** a handy acronym to summarize motivational factors tied to both fulfillment and love–hate–greed; stands for money, opportunity, values, ego, and revenge.

**Negative question:** one designed to confuse, for example, "Are you not going to the annual conference?"

**Nontopic question:** casual and off-topic question.

**OSINT:** an abbreviation for open-source intelligence; refers to the source of the information.

**Organizer:** sees value in the system and believes in positive action to accomplish a goal within the system but has little patience.

**Personal extinction:** death of a personality through the destruction or violation of self-defining traits.

**PHOTINT:** an abbreviation for photo intelligence; refers to the source of the information.

**Polygrapher:** an interrogator armed with a sensitive electronic instrument.

**Preamble phrases:** words, sounds, or phrases inserted to buy time as your brain tries to configure an answer to a question, for example, "There is so much to consider . . ."

**Prepared question:** see "canned question."

**Priority intelligence requirements (PIRs):** information you truly need.

**Rapport:** framework for information transfer.

**Regulators:** movements to manage another person's speech.

**Repeat question:** same as a previous question but asked in a different way.

**Revolutionaries:** have no patience when it comes to change and see the entire status quo as the issue.

**SIGINT:** an abbreviation for signal intelligence; refers to the source of the information.

**SITREP:** an abbreviation for situation report.

**Source leads:** information a source drops into a conversation that the questioner thinks is worth pursuing.

**Subroutines:** processes and practices repeated so often that they become automatic.

**Top-grading:** upgrading your team by eliminating low performers and cultivating, attracting, and retaining high performers.

**Transformers:** are like revolutionaries with patience; they see the current system as needing overhaul but will take a gradual approach to change.

**Trip wire:** sets off a device without the need for human intervention; also a mechanism for prodding a person to action.

**Vague question:** one with multiple interpretations possible, for example, "Did you see them doing that?"

**Value planning:** viewing decisions as building blocks; decisions build toward further action, adding value to your next step.

# INDEX